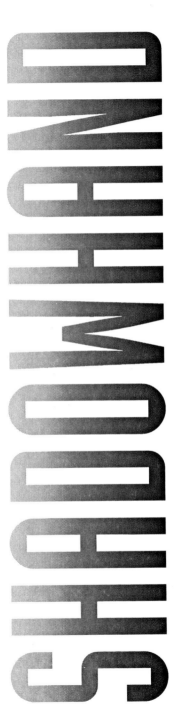

To Sue Dillon Daniel Anderson

SHADOWHAND

The History and Secrets of Ninja Taisavaki

Dr. Haha Lung &
Christopher B. Prowant

Paladin Press • Boulder, Colorado

STE* C 1

Also by Dr. Haha Lung:

The Ancient Art of Strangulation
Assassin!: The Deadly Art of the Cult of the Assassins
Knights of Darkness: Secrets of the World's Deadliest Night Fighters
The Black Science: Ancient and Modern Techniques of
   Ninja Mind Manipulation (with Christopher B. Prowant)

Shadowhand: The History and Secrets of Ninja Taisavaki
by Dr. Haha Lung and Christopher Prowant

Copyright © 2000 by Dr. Haha Lung and Christopher Prowant

ISBN 1-58160-071-2
Printed in the United States of America

Published by Paladin Press, a division of
Paladin Enterprises, Inc.
Gunbarrel Tech Center
7077 Winchester Circle
Boulder, Colorado 80301 USA
+1.303.443.7250

Direct inquiries and/or orders to the above address.

PALADIN, PALADIN PRESS, and the "horse head" design
are trademarks belonging to Paladin Enterprises and
registered in United States Patent and Trademark Office.

Illustrations by Ralph Dean Omar

Visit our Web site at www.paladin-press.com

TABLE OF

Contents

The Upperhand of Shadowhand

Survival is a continual search for ever better ways to outwit our enemies.

How advantageous it would be if, rather than having to go toe to toe with a foe, we could approach that enemy unseen, strike that enemy a telling blow he never sees coming, and then disappear back into the shadows.

Classic guerrilla strategy; classic ninja tactic.

Through the ages, numerous individuals and groups worldwide developed strategies and tactics designed to render themselves and their attacks invisible to their enemies—techniques that allowed them to disguise their intent while misdirecting the attention of their foes. Some of these techniques were based on sound physical principles, for example the study of eye mechanics (blind spots and other inherent weaknesses in the mind's eye).

Other groups became masters of using camouflage and body kinetics to disguise form and movement in order to trick an enemy's eye and confuse his mind.

Still others are credited with discovering mystical methods of shape-shifting and "true" invisibility.

Beyond all the secrecy, speculation, and superstition surrounding these shadowy groups (disinformation more often than not spread by the groups themselves), what we do know is that all these killer cadres developed ingenious methods of silent movement, as well as the ability to disguise their intent, permitting them to strike into the unguarded heart of an enemy before that enemy ever suspected Death's cold "shadowhand" was upon him.

While these shadowy cadres understandably did their best to keep their secrets to themselves, inevitably, their secret techniques designed to give them the upper hand over their foes were either spied or pried away from them.

For serious martial artists and survivalists, the tactics and techniques of *all* these groups deserve scrutiny. However, there are only 24 hours in a day, and to study all these groups would consume more than one lifetime. Fortunately, the most accomplished of all these killers, the shinobi ninja of medieval Japan, were also the best documented.

Among the ninja, tactics and techniques permitting agents to disguise their intent so as to get close enough to an enemy to cut him down—to strike an enemy with unseen blows and then escape the scene unscathed—are known as *taisavaki*, "the shadowhand."

Enemies unfortunate enough to feel the icy touch of this shadowhand grip their hearts never rose again.

PART I

Appreciation:
Masters in the Shadows

Before we can begin our application of the shadowhand techniques that allowed former masters of the shadows to survive and accomplish their missions, it is vital that we first get an appreciation for these shadow masters and their deadly art. It is important to understand these individuals and groups and what motivated them.

It is also important to get a glimpse into the times they thrived in, the trials and turmoil that gave them the choice to adapt or die. For these were the forces that drove them to search far afield for ever more devastating techniques of stealth, secrecy, and subterfuge, all of which helped give birth to the shadowhand.

CHAPTER ONE

Shadow Walkers

Since ancient times, sundry shamans and magicians have used legerdemain to dazzle crowds, while unscrupulous con artists have adroitly used sleight of hand to separate gullible victims from their purses.

Likewise, history abounds with individuals and groups who sought to wrap themselves in secrecy, stealth, and skulduggery. Their motivation and methods varied greatly. Some cloaked themselves in shadows for personal gain; others were moved by political or religious fervor. Yet, beneath it all, all of these shadow walkers had the same agenda: secrecy first, survival a close second, and the slaying of their enemies a sacred third. Some developed techniques of their own, while others embraced and updated the tricks of ancient shamans and past charlatans. Even when they did not embrace the actual practices of former shadow walkers, still these killer cadres literally took to heart—their enemies' heart—the "shadowhand" principle, giving their already deadly killing arts an even more lethal edge.

In the west, many Native American warrior lodges were renowned (and feared) for their methods of deceptive strategy and silent slaying, whether drawing a superior enemy force into an ambush (just ask Custer) or engaging in a hand-to-hand struggle.

In Dark Ages northern Europe, wolfshirt warriors (i.e., viking "ninja," stealth-oriented companions to the dread berserkers) employed similar deceptions to give their warrior bands the upper hand. Wolfshirts called this kind of strategy "glamour" ("to dazzle an enemy's eyes; to make an enemy see what is not there; to hide what is there").

Many of these ancient wolfshirt techniques survived into the Middle Ages and were revived and revised by the Order of Knights Templar.

Crusading Knights Templar were also believed to have learned shadowy methods of fighting and spying from murderous Middle Eastern cultists known as *hashishin*, from whence comes our word "assassin" (Lung 1997).

Across the Far East, numerous groups plied the assassin's trade for profit and/or promoted bloody secretive traditions, detaching themselves from the shadows only long enough to cut down a foe with an unseen blow before disappearing back into those shadows.

In India there were the thuggee worshippers of dark goddess Kali (Lung 1995).

Tibet had its elusive sdop sdop, warrior-monks, seen only when they chose to be seen.

And in imperial China there were the moshuh nanren, in hindsight dubbed "the ninja of China." Moshuh nanren were specially trained operatives dedicated to the safety of the emperor and to Chinese royalty.

A cross between the Gestapo and the Navy SEALS, moshuh nanren acted as bodyguards to Chinese royalty while ruthlessly rooting out and eliminating any threat to the throne.

Perpetuating the popular superstition that they were descended from *lin kuei* ("forest demons"), moshuh nanren specialized in making enemies vanish without a trace and killing foes without leaving a mark. This led to the widespread belief that moshuh nanren possessed the secret of *dim mak* ("death's touch"), a belief moshuh nanren did nothing to discourage (Omar 1989).

As one scheming royal faction gained the upper hand over its rivals, those who moshuh nanren agents thought were still loyal to the overthrown faction were ruthlessly hunted down and executed. As a result, surviving "homeless" moshuh nanren helped found many of China's more ruthless secret societies, while moshuh nanren fleeing abroad helped spread the their version of "shadowhand" to other Asian countries.

Medieval Korea had the hawang-do warriors, its own cadre of deadly fighters with their own expertise in both night fighting and striking foes down with seldom-seen strikes (Lung 1998).

Meanwhile, Vietnam had its "black flag" assassins, forerunners of Vietcong "sappers."

In Indonesia, travelers had to beware of infamous "nightsiders"—assassins silently slipping from the shadows to cut throats, catching the hapless victim's purse before it hit the ground and, just as quickly, melting back into the dark.

Specific Eastern unarmed fighting styles also used deceptive stances, movements, and strikes. Indonesian silat is famed for this.

Chinese styles of wushu (kung fu) fighting are also noted for their use of deceptive movement. For example, monkey-style kung fu employs low-to-the-ground stances to break up shape and silhouette ("The Three We See," Chapter 4). Likewise, tiger-style kung fu uses "'oblique" strikes—strikes designed to draw an opponent right while attacking in from the left. (Taijutsu is discussed fully in Part II.)

Fortunately for us (unfortunate for their foes!), all these methods—from the mystical to the purely manipulative—were collected, catalogued, and used by one deadly group, the ninja of Japan.

CHAPTER TWO

The Ninja Shadowhand

The Japanese ninja, more correctly known as *shinobi*, became so adept at collecting and perfecting methods of stealthy movement and fighting that theirs became a martial art all to itself, albeit an "art" that never lost its lethal martial edge. This was the art of taisavaki, "the shadowhand.

ORIGINS OF THE NINJA

When it comes to the history of the Japanese ninja, it is hard to separate fact from fiction. This is made doubly difficult since ninja went out of their way to perpetuate rumors and myths about themselves, not the least of which was their ability to strike a foe with an unseen "shadowhand."

The Myth

Ninja trace themselves back to the storm god Susano, who is credited with the planting of the great forests of Japan's main island Honshu. Susano sprang from the right eye of Izanagi, sibling of Izanami; Izanagi and Izanami are the divine brother and sister creators of the Japanese islands. Susano, in turn, is responsible for the birth of the *tengu*, half-man/half-bird *kinjin* ("goblins") who haunt the great forests of Japan.

Tengu live in clans ruled by a chieftain. Sometimes *tengu* are black, other times red. They wear cloaks (made of feathers, leaves, straw) and sport small black hats. *Tengu* are great swordsmen and possess magical powers, including shape-shifting and invisibility.

Japanese mythology relates how 12th-century samurai hero Minimoto Yoshitsune (aka Ushiwara) learned his swordsmanship and combat tactics while being hidden by a clan of tengu. Ushiwara's longtime companion Benkei (aka Oni-waka, "Demon Youth") was himself half-tengu.

Ushiwara's story is a thinly disguised tale for the fact that Japan's greatest cultural hero was forced to seek refuge with the despised "ninja" clans of central Japan after the defeat of his clan in the early part of the 12th century CE (Common Era).

Whether the medieval ninja of Japan actually believed themselves descended from the very gods that created their islands via the demonic tengu, or whether they merely perpetuated this myth for outsiders and potential enemies, is moot. The ninja's being associated in their enemy's mind with both the divine and the devilish served its purpose: promoting the awe and fear in which the ninja were held.

The Fact

The actual origins of the Japanese ninja can be traced back to a 6th-century CE rogue named Otomono-Saijin, better known as Shinobi ("One Who Sneaks In"). Otomo was employed as a spy for Prince Shotoku during the latter's struggle for the imperial throne.

Where Otomo acquired his skills is not known for certain.

Like most accomplished spies, he undoubtedly gleaned his "ninja" techniques from a variety of sources available in Japan at the time, discarding the superfluous and embracing and expanding on what worked.

Possible sources of such information at the time included techniques from as far afield as India and Korea, and even Tibet and China.

The most likely source of information was mainland China and included arriving texts and teachers willing to share their secrets. Among these were Chinese military classics such as Sun Tzu's *Ping-fa* (*The Art of War*).

Other martial arts and spying techniques were gleaned from Buddhist monks and perhaps displaced moshuh nanren agents—either fleeing from China or infiltrating Japan on missions of their own.

Due to constant fighting between rival samurai factions, Japanese "ninja" techniques continued to develop. However, at this time, anyone using stealth and skulduggery (e.g., criminal, spy) was considered "ninja."

The word "ninja" comes from the Japanese written character for *shinobi* and, in medieval times, was applied generically to all those—from sundry criminals to master spies—who used stealth, secrecy, and subterfuge to accomplish their goals.

The 14th century saw a major increase in "ninja" activity as "ninja" criminal gangs took advantage of the chaos caused by warring samurai to rob and plunder.

At the same time, every would-be "ninja" spy peeked out and peddled information to the highest bidder. This century also saw the rise of true ninja, in the form of the great shinobi clans in the central Japanese provinces of Iga and Koga.

Eventually these highly organized ninja groups numbered over 50 separate clans and schools (*ryu*), making the region a near autonomous state.

Some of these great clans had been formed by *yamabushi* ("mountain warriors"), Buddhist and cultist monks displaced after the destruction of their temples.

Other ninja schools, the *kusunoki-ryu*, for example, were

founded by bands of *ronin*, samurai who had lost their feudal lords and all their holdings in the internecine fighting (Lung 1997).

Truth be known, most of these ninja clans wanted simply to be left alone. Others, however, actively warred against regional samurai lords (*daimyo*) or hired themselves out as spies and mercenaries, playing one samurai faction against the other.

It was during this medieval period that "true" ninjutsu (art of the ninja) came into its own, with the great ninja clans perfecting its dark and deadly craft.

THE NINE TRAINING HALLS OF NINJUTSU

Traditional ninjutsu is divided into nine areas of training known as "halls." Each of these halls, while distinct in itself, overlaps with and complements the other eight for a rounded course of study. Ninja trainees first familiarize themselves with all nine halls before specializing in a particular hall. Over the course of a lifetime, a dedicated ninja will master several, if not all nine, halls. Although each hall is separate, each has as its basis the concept of the shadowhand: techniques whose specific focus is to help the ninja to remain undetected until striking, strike unseen, and then "vanish" from sight, surviving to strike another day. Each of the nine halls is described below.

Unarmed Combat
At this level, mastery of a basic course of unarmed hand-to-hand fighting is required. Ninja students are then encouraged to study any and all other styles of martial arts available, gleaning from each any technique that might be useful.

When examining other styles of fighting, ninja students are taught to be especially alert for techniques that qualify as "shadowhand," or those aiding the ninja in striking unseen. (Taijutsu is discussed fully in Part II.)

Combat with Wooden Weapons
Various wooden weapons (e.g., loo-staff, go-short sticks, nunchaku) are taught at this level. Here, ninja learn valuable

shadowhand ploys for disguising the fact that they are carrying weapons. (See the section on kobudo-jutsu in Part II.)

Combat with Blade Weapons

Here the ninja student masters the use of blade weapons such as sword, knife, *shuriken* (throwing stars), and *kama* (sickle). Again, students are taught to pay special attention to various shadowhand techniques intended to disguise the carrying and use of blade weapons.

Combat with Flexible Weapons

Flexible weapons (e.g., chains, ropes, scarves) are mastered in this hall, along with shadowhand strategies for hiding and then employing them effectively. (See the section on kobudo-jutsu in Part II.)

Specialized Combat Training

Specialized movements (e.g., rolling, rebounding, shifting and disguising body movement) are mastered at this level. (See Taijutsu, Part II.) Here the student learns to apply the concept of the shadowhand to all the tactics and techniques taught him so far.

The Art of Disguise

At this level students learn a variety of methods for disguising themselves (e.g., false ID, role playing). Most important, students learn shadowhand techniques for disguising their movement and distorting their shape and silhouette to allow them to approach a foe undetected.

The Art of Espionage

In this hall, students master specific skills designed to aid them in the twofold goal of espionage: first, the gathering of intelligence, and then—when necessary—assassination.

The Art of Escape and Evasion

At this level, ninja must learn not only to escape physical

restraints but also to master the shadowhand techniques that permit them to escape from capture and elude pursuers.

The Art of Mysticism

By understanding the beliefs and superstitions of foes, ninja are able to use mental shadowhand techniques to trick a foe's mind into seeing what is not there and missing what is there—namely, the ninja!

The most important thing to remember is that the principle of shadowhand applies to all nine halls. Adding shadowhand ploys and positioning to already effective martial arts technique is like adding a coating of deadly poison to an already keen blade.

CHAPTER THREE

Taisavaki-jutsu (Art of Avoidance)

Avoid being seen; seen, avoid capture; captured, avoid being held.
—Shadowhand credo

It is always best to avoid confrontation. However, when combat is unavoidable it is preferable to strike a foe from behind or from an oblique, unexpected angle. Confronting a foe face to face, it is best to strike with blows one's foe never sees coming. Having struck such sure and sudden blows, one should then escape the scene as quickly as possible.

The strategy and the skills required to accomplish this ideal was known to the shinobi ninja as taisavaki-jutsu, literally "the art of avoidance" or, more simply, "the shadowhand."

Taisavaki-jutsu includes all strategies, tactics, and techniques that allow one to remain hidden until striking, to strike unseen, and then, having struck the enemy, to elude capture and make good one's escape.

For a technique to qualify as "shadowhand" it must aid in the accomplishment of one or more of four criteria:

- Shadowhand technique aids the practitioner in remaining undetected, even when surrounded by enemies. This is known as inno-jutsu (the art of hiding).

- Shadowhand technique allows the practitioner to strike down a foe suddenly and safely, before the latter's arrival on the scene is even suspected.

- Once combat is joined, shadowhand technique enables the practitioner to misdirect his opponent and then strike with unexpected and unseen blows

- When necessary, shadowhand technique allows the practitioner to "vanish" from the scene and elude any pursuers. This is inton-jutsu (the art of escape and evasion).

Many techniques from many different schools and styles of martial arts fit these four criteria and, thus, qualify as shadowhand. The more of these shadowhand techniques the martial artist can isolate and master—no matter from what school of survival they originate—the better will be his or her overall defensive and offensive arsenal:

Not restricting oneself to a particular style of fighting was one of the major strengths of medieval ninja and should be one of the main training objectives of the contemporary street Ninja.

—Dirk Skinner
Street Ninja, 1995

When setting out to master the shadowhand, the most important thing is that the student first and foremost internalizes the concept of the shadowhand, as opposed to simply learning various techniques and repeating them by rote. Mastering the concept of the shadowhand requires that the student obtain and then hone a talent for improvising. The ability to "think on our feet," to adjust instantly to changing circumstance, is the hallmark of the shadowhand.

Nothing will get you killed more quickly than hesitating and/or being predictable. Therefore, before you learn the specific techniques offered in Part II of this book, it is important that you first understand the basics of how human beings actually "see."

Comprehending how your enemy "sees" the world around him is the first step in making him see what you want him to see—and preventing him from seeing what you don't want him to see.

CHAPTER FOUR

The Basics of Seeing

Once we understand how the eye gets its information, it is a simple matter to confuse an enemy's eye into misinterpreting incoming information.

—Dr. Haha Lung
Knights of Darkness, 1998

How we see the world extends far beyond merely seeing with the organ of the eye. Accomplished warriors train to "see" with the whole of their being. (See the disscussion of peripheral body awareness, p. 36.) However, for the purpose of shadowhand, understanding "seeing" begins with understanding the physical eye.

In his *Street Ninja*, Dirk Skinner drills into the reader that the more one knows about how the human body is put together, the easier it is to take it apart!

This holds true for the eye as well.

The better one's understanding of how the eye is put together, the easier it is to confuse the eye and ultimately blind it physically and psychologically.

THE THREE WE SEE

At its most basic, shadowhand uses tricks and techniques designed to distort information coming into the eye in order to confuse and mislead the easily distracted eye. "Seeing" occurs when light rays pass through the cornea and lens and enter the eye, striking the inner surface of the eye (the retina). The retina gathers light-bytes of information and sends them in the form of electrical signals into the brain via the optic nerve.

Once in the brain, these bytes of information are "reassembled" and we see.

Receptors in the retina are known as rods and cones. Each human eye contains about 120 million rods and 6 million cones. Near the center of the retina is a round area called the macula, consisting chiefly of cones. The macula's job is to produce a sharp image of scenes at which the eyes are directly aimed, especially in bright light. These same cones also allow us to see color. The rest of the retina provides peripheral vision (PV), our ability to see objects to the side while looking straight ahead. Most of the rods lie in this part of the eye. (See Figure 1.)

In addition to giving us PV, rods also contain a pigment called rhodopsin ("visual purple") that enables the eye to distinguish shades of gray and to see in dim light.

When exposed to a bright light, especially at night, the eye is "wiped clean" of rhodopsin. It then takes 10 to 40 minutes for visual purple to renew itself, depending on how bright the light the eye was exposed to.

Eyes become adjusted to bright light much more quickly than they do to darkness. Adapting to darkness takes from 30 minutes to an hour. For an in-depth examination on how light and darkness affect human beings, as well as how light and darkness can be purposely deployed to affect a foe, see Haha Lung (1998).

Movement

Constantly besieged by foes (samurai and rival ninja clans), the shinobi-ninja children were taught vital survival skills before they could walk. One of the most important lessons was conveyed in the parable of Daruma and the parrot.

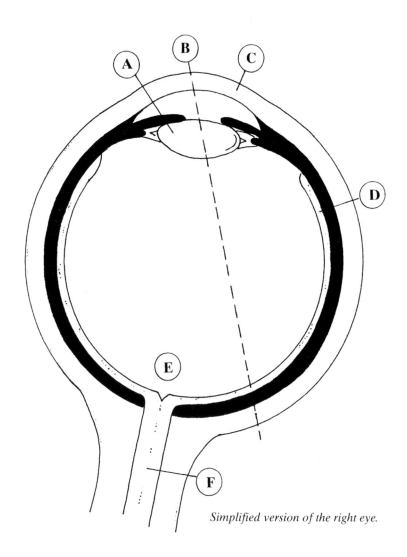

Simplified version of the right eye.

FIGURE 1: THE HUMAN EYE

A. *Lens*
B. *Visual axis*
C. *Cornea*
D. *Retina*
E. *"Blind spot," aka "optic disk"*
F. *Optic nerve*

While traveling in China, Zen founder Daruma came across a parrot held in a gilded cage. "Master Daruma," the parrot pleaded, "Can your Zen method show me how to free myself from my cruel owner?"

Taken by the bird's sincere plea, Daruma told him, "In order to be free, you must meditate by sitting as still as possible, slow your breathing, and clear your mind of all thought."

After Daruma left him, the parrot did as instructed.

As soon as the bird's cruel owner returned home he saw his favorite pet lying motionless in its cage!

Rushing to the cage, the owner opened the cage door and took the motionless bird in the open palm of his hand ... at which point the bird suddenly came "back to life" and flew away!

Through this parable, shinobi children were taught both the value of meditation and the importance of remaining motionless to outwit a foe.

Since the eye first sees movement, remaining motionless is the best way to avoid detection. The human eye's ability to detect movement instantly is a vital survival skill. However, this same ability is used in shadowhand to manipulate—by drawing or distracting—a foe's attention.

Whenever two objects are seen together and one moves while the other remains motionless, our eye instinctually follows the moving object. Knowledge of this human habit allows us to remain motionless while drawing the onlooker's eye away from what we don't want him to look at. (See Figure 2.) This is the bread and butter of the professional magician's trade, from the simplest of slight of hand to making the Statue of Liberty "disappear."

The tendency of the human eye to follow movement is also the basis of the most successful of shadowhand techniques. Being the magicians that they are, shadowhand practitioners use movement

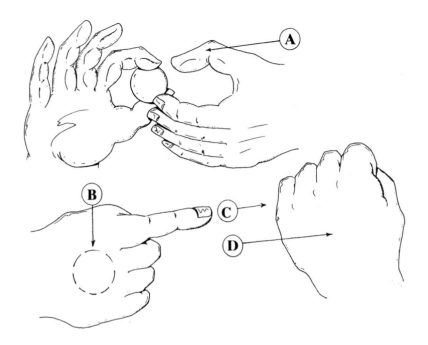

FIGURE 2: SLEIGHT OF HAND

A. As the second hand "closes" around the object (e.g., coin, ball) held by
    the first hand . . .
B. . . . the object drops unseen into the palm of the first hand.
C. The index finger of the first hand misdirects the eye of the observer by
    pointing to the second hand, while . . .
D. . . . the eye of the observer naturally follows the moving second hand.

to draw an onlooker's attention away from what is really going on.

    This is the most basic of military strategies: feign an attack
at the enemy's front gate, drawing off his forces, while slipping
sappers over his back wall.

---

*Knowing the art of the direct and the indirect approach, you will always be
victorious.*

—Sun Tzu

In the most classic of guerilla ploys, a squad of guerillas makes a halfhearted attack and then flees in the face of a superior enemy force, drawing the pursuing force into a larger (and waiting motionless) ambush by guerrillas.

Likewise, locked in personal combat, the accomplished martial artist feigns blows to one part of an opponent's body before striking a telling blow to another point (see Figure 3). Many martial arts styles (e.g., tiger-style kung fu), specialize in "oblique" strikes wherein they shift outside while striking inside. (See the discussions of unarmed/armed combat in Part II.)

FIGURE 3: OBLIQUE STRIKING

A. *Having moved to the outside of your foe's right leading punch by employing a "cross-body block" . . .*

B. *. . . strike back into your foe using a variety of "oblique" counterstrikes (e.g., backfist, hammerfist, shuto)*

Shadow, Shape, and Silhouette

For about half the day there is darkness, so unless you plan to spend half the day hiding, hoping the night doesn't seep in under your door, it might be a good idea to learn how to use the night and the shadows to your advantage.

—Dirk Skinner
Street Ninja, 1995

Having spotted movement, we immediately try to make sense of it by associating what we see (or think we saw) with known objects capable of movement (e.g., the human shape, which is two-legged and vertically oriented, versus the horizontally oriented four-legged shape of an animal).

Humans have an easily identifiable five points of silhouette shape consisting of our head, legs, and arms. Drawing in one or more of these five points of reference distorts our silhouette, making it harder for an observer to pick us out from our background and/or from similarly shaped objects. For example, simply turning to the side distorts our body outline, making it more difficult to distinguish. (See Figure 4.)

Likewise, by kneeling, lowering his head to his chest, and holding his arms close to his sides, a man can make his silhouette indistinguishable from a trash can in a darkened alley or a boulder in an open field. (See Figure 5.)

Martial artists and accomplished killer cadres all understand the importance of masking shape and silhouette.

Ninja practiced to distort their shape in order to evade detection, often sporting small cloaks that they could drape over themselves to further help distort their outline. Ninja movements in combat, whether during guerrilla operations or during personal combat, were designed to shift and distort the ninja's shape to confuse the enemy's eye as much and as often as possible.

So successful were these ninja shadowhand tactics and techniques that to this day tales are told of the ninja's magical abilities to "shape shift" and in turn "disappear." (See Chapter 5: The Quest for Invisibility.)

FIGURE 4: SHIFTING SILHOUETTE

A. *Full figure facing foreward, all body reference points (head, arms, legs) easily discernible.*

B. *Side view of same figure in silhouette (with camouflage leaves) as small tree.*

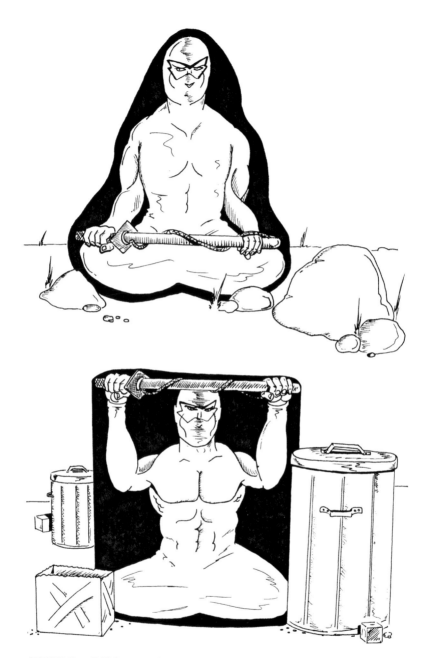

FIGURE 5: DISGUISING SHAPE AND SILHOUETTE

FIGURE 6: "ALIGNED" STANCE

Conversely, Westerners are raised on the ideal of two opponents standing "toe to toe," whether in sports (football, boxing, wrestling) or in more dangerous pursuits (gunfighting, armies at war). In personal combat, such a face-to-face ("aligned") stance keeps all five points of the human body visible: the head (a main target) and the legs and arms (main weapons used).

With head and shoulders aligned (A) and with feet aligned (B), all five body reference points (head, arms, legs) are easily discernible (Figure 6).

This is why untrained Western fighters often find themselves at a loss when facing fighters trained in Eastern martial arts strategy, especially those martial artists adroit at using fighting stances and oblique shifting footwork deliberately designed to distort the five points on the body an opponent uses for reference (See Figure 7). This is especially true of the more esoteric-looking Chinese "animal forms" of kung fu, for example, monkey style.

To master one's forces, remain shapeless in the eye of the enemy. In this way, the wiliest of spies (k'ai ho) *cannot slip in, nor the wisest of generals make successful plans against you.*

—Sun Tzu

Color

After movement and silhouette, the eye sees color. Three types of pigment in retina cones make it possible for us to see color. Cyanolabe allows us to see blue light; chlorolabe, green light; and erythrolabe, red. Collectively, these pigments enable us to distinguish more than 200 colors.

Keeping track of the constant interplay and shifting of this dazzling array of colors can easily mislead the eye. Stage magicians routinely distract their audience with scantily clad assistants wearing dazzling sequined costumes, in contrast to the magician's own dark clothing. Other times, magicians sport colorful robes easily discarded in favor of black clothing that allows them (and/or their assistants) to move against the dark background of the stage unnoticed by the audience.

FIGURE 7: DISGUISED FIGHTING STANCE

A.   *Squatting posture throws off foe's "line of sight." (See Figures 8–10.)*
B.   *Hands held close to body in line with the silhouette distort the five points of body reference, making it harder for a foe to keep track of them.*

To trick the eye with color, ninja often wore reversible robes that allowed them to more easily lose themselves in a crowd. Modern "ninja" sport reversible jackets and different-color wigs and hats. In a field operation, a ninja could disguise a lighter colored horse with darker dye easily washed off in an emergency (Lung 1998: 82). The modern equivalent of this would be to paint a getaway car with water-soluble paint.

TO SEE OR NOT TO SEE

We worldly men have miserable, mad, mistaking eyes.

—Shakespeare
Titus Andronicus

Several factors determine when we see and, more important, what we see and how accurately we see it. All too often what we end up "seeing" is totally different from what is actually there.

Factors influencing how accurately we "see" include our field of vision and any physical and/or psychological "blind spots" we have.

Field of Vision

Our field of vision (FOV) refers to everything that we see straight ahead and to the sides as we look steadily at any object. Our FOV is composed of our line of sight (LOS) and our PV.

Line of Sight

Untrained human beings seldom bother to look either up or down. Instead, we look at the world at a level that is constant—the level of our eyes—unless something catches our attention (e.g., a noise or movement that draws our attention either up or down). (See Figure 8.)

In addition to our actual physical range of LOS, we all have psychological LOS factors that affect the accuracy of our seeing. For example, we seldom think about what is above our head or below our feet.

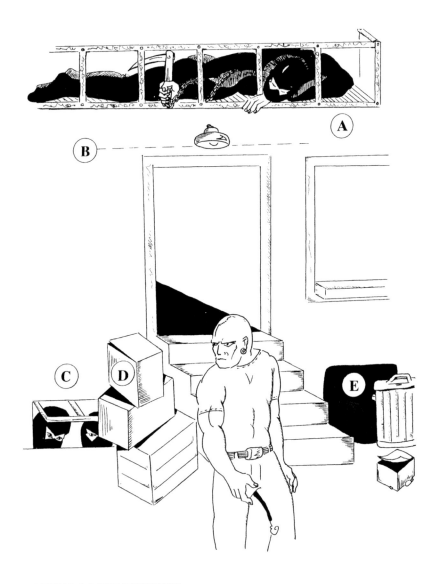

FIGURE 8: LINE OF SIGHT

A. *Unless our attention is drawn up, we seldom look up.*
B. *Whenever possible, always hide above the "sight line" (Lung 1998).*
C. *Likewise, unless our attention is drawn downward we seldom look down.*
D. *See Figure 16.*
E. *See Figure 5.*

Ninja recognized the limitations of LOS long ago and used it to their advantage, developing strategies that allowed them to slip in under an enemy's LOS (e.g., through sewers, on the undercarriage of vehicles, by digging under walls), or else go over it, for example by moving above the "sight line" on the ledges and roofs of buildings, above the glare made by passing vehicles, street lights and neon signs (Lung 1998: 88). Ninja are notorious for hiding unnoticed for days in a castle's rafters, just above an enemy's head, waiting for the right time to strike. (See Figure 9.)

In one instance, a ninja assassin waited patiently for several days under the waste hole in a Shogun's toilet in order to slay the tyrant when he answered the call of Nature (Lung 1998: 113).

When it came to personal combat, ninja always approached an enemy sentry from behind, by crouching under their LOS, often augmenting this with a variation of "the oldest trick in the book" designed to draw off the sentry's attention.

Likewise, ninja used any overhang to their advantage (e.g.,

FIGURE 9: APPROACHING SENTRY UNDER LINE OF SIGHT

tree limbs, rafters, fire escapes, ledges) both to hide while spying out intelligence and for techniques designed to strike silently from above.

Peripheral Vision

PV is the ability to perceive movement at the edges of our vision field (i.e., "out of the corner of our eye"). PV sees only in black and white, since the area responsible for peripheral vision is controlled by color-blind rods. Any decrease in overall light helps increase PV. Thus, narrowing our eyes, deliberately restricting the amount of light coming into the eye, helps increase our PV.

Awareness and cultivation of PV are vital survival skills, not just for the professional warrior but also for the average person waiting at an ATM. Fortunately, we can improve our PV through deliberate practice (Lung 1998: 55).

Uncommon "Sense"

If it "feels" wrong, it probably is. What would you rather do, have to chide yourself for "over-reacting," or have to pay the doctor for under-reacting, for not having listened to your sixth sense?

—Dirk Skinner,
Street Ninja, 1995

The goals are survival and overcoming foes. The means to accomplish these goals is to master full use of ourselves. This means not limiting ourselves to "seeing" with only our all-too-fallible eyes alone. Awareness of the world around us only begins with the eye. We must then extend our awareness by using all our senses to "see." Inevitably, full use of our five physical senses will give the impression to others—those less aware, those less inclined toward practice and improvement of self—that we have "ESP."

Many people are convinced that human beings do have an "extra" sense—one that warns them of danger. Ninja called this ability *taiharagei*, body awareness. The anecdotal evidence

FIGURE 10: ABOVE/BELOW LINE-OF-SIGHT ATTACKS

A. No matter what their surroundings, shadowhanders can turn the LOS
    failing against their foes.

that some people do seem to possess an uncanny ability to "sense" when others are approaching or even watching from afar is indeed intriguing. Some seem born with this "gift," while others—shadowhanders, for example—actively cultivate this ability.

Various explanations have been given for this phenomenon. One plausible scientific explanation is that the electromagnetic (EM) field surrounding one human body (varying in expanse from person to person) recognizes when another person's EM field touches it. Others maintain that this ability to sense when someone is approaching is merely the subconscious mind perceiving below-audible sounds, slight vibrations in the ground, and subtle pheromone scents.

For purposes of survival—for mastery of the shadowhand—all argument regarding this matter is moot. Only results matter. So long as an ability or skill, innate or acquired, increases our chances of surviving and ultimately stepping on the throat of our enemy, it is an edge worth honing and one we must be willing to wield without hesitation.

Peripheral body sense ("body awareness") refers to our ability to sense when someone is within three to five feet of us. Each of us has this ability, which appears to be inborn, although for most of us the daily rigmarole of modern society has blunted it (as it has our appreciation of our other senses). Few human beings, however, take the time to appreciate and/or actively cultivate this body awareness.

A man may see how this world goes with no eyes.

—Shakespeare
King Lear

Warriors often learn the hard way that in personal combat there are times when their eyes are useless, when they must rely on one or more of their other senses to save them.

When there is little or no light to activate their eyes, or when danger creeps up from behind or waits in ambush above or below their LOS, or when menace lurks beyond the edges of their PV, they must rely on their other senses to save them.

Given proper attention, the sense of smell can detect an approaching enemy's deodorant (or lack thereof); hearing can perceive the subtle sound of sand beneath his foot. Likewise, skin is sensitive to hot and cold, subtle changes in the wind and barometric pressure, and vibrations from myriad sources. The skin of the fingertips and face can perceive pressure that depresses the skin a mere .00004 inch.

Martial artists (especially grapplers such as jujutsu practitioners) rely to a great extent on their sense of touch to warn them of an opponent's next move (shifting balance, attempting to establish a lock). Sense of touch is important, not only when fighting in pitch darkness, but also when in a well-lit life-or-death struggle. Locked in close-quarters combat, one cannot always see an opponent move his limbs (e.g., shift his feet). It is therefore imperative to learn to "feel" an opponent's shifting his weight in preparation for a throw or an inside knee strike to the groin in order to defend against it.

Likewise, when counterattacking, accomplished fighters train their bodies to respond to the touch (resistance) of an opponent's blocking arm instantly. This allows them to reroute their blow to a secondary target (rather than having to withdraw it and recock it).

As you will see in the section on unarmed combat, shadowhanders must master this ability to recognize an enemy's intention from touch alone, not only to better protect themselves on the shifting sands of combat, but also to turn the tide against their enemy.

* * * * *

Despite technological developments, nothing is better than developing your own innate senses and abilities.

—Dr. Haha Lung
Knights of Darkness, 1998

Physical Blind Spots

Having taken time to understand how the eye sees, let's turn our attention to those physical and psychological factors that can prevent us from seeing accurately, and, more important, those "blind spots" we can use to unbalance and overcome an enemy.

The Optic Disk

In every human eye there is a small area of blindness that interferes with the eye's normal field of vision. This is known as the "blind spot." This blind spot occurs on the nasal side of the retina (toward the nose) where the optic nerve enters the eyeball. There is no vision in this area because there is no retina (inner layer of the eyeball) there (see Figure 1).

To test for your blind spot, keep your left eye closed while looking at the cross below:

Now move the book backward and forward. When it is about six inches away from your face, the black circle will disappear when its image aligns with the optic disk—your eye's physical blind spot. You generally don't notice your eyes' blind spots because, with binocular vision, the other eye compensates for its companion eye. (NOTE: Changes in the size and shape of the blind spots give doctors vital information on diseases such as glaucoma and brain tumors.)

The moshuh nanren, the "ninja" of imperial China, were rumored to possess a technique of moving that permitted them to remain invisible to a foe, even when approaching that foe from the front. It has been speculated that this technique involved intuitively remaining in an opponent's blind spot. Others argue that this would be impossible because for a man with two perfectly functioning eyes (binocular vision), one eye always compensates for the blind spot of the other. Like the true *dim-mak* "touch of death" used by the moshuh nanren, the validity of this invisble approach may never be known. (See Chapter 5: The Quest for Invisibility.)

Point of View

When near, make an enemy believe you are far away. Far away, make an enemy imagine you are near.

—Sun Tzu

A Japanese riddle told to children asks, How can your thumb make a mountain disappear? Unacquainted with perspective and "point of view," children are amazed when you show them how (from their perspective at least) their raised thumb is indeed bigger than a mountain. (See Figure 11.)

This may seem like a simple child's misunderstanding of perspective, yet stage magicians routinely use this same principle to awe audiences. One popular TV magician recently amazed his audience by making a "herd" of elephants (closer to three or four!) disappear from the middle of the desert using this same principle.

Having shown the television audience the herd standing in the middle of the desert, the magician drew the camera recording the illusion back through a puppeteer's small frame-stage. As the curtains were drawn, temporarily obscuring the "herd," the frame-stage was slightly shifted to the right so that the thin border of the stage obscured the elephants when the curtain was pulled aside (Figure 12).

What we see depends on our perspective, our point of view (POV). Ninja know this.

Using this same "thumb hides mountain" principle, a ninja operative (disguised as a confused drunk, a monk, or a beautiful girl) can temporarily obscure the vision of a sentry in order to allow his confederate to slip by unnoticed (Figure 13).

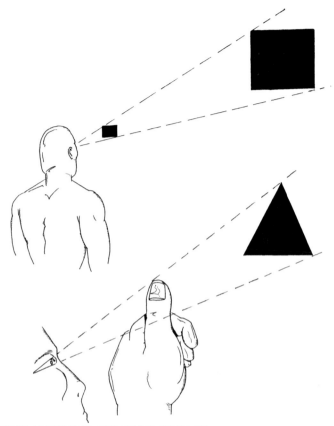

FIGURE 11: THUMB HIDES MOUNTAIN

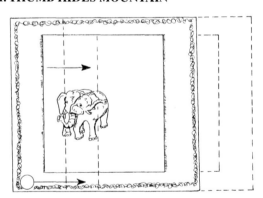

FIGURE 12: DISAPPEARING ELEPHANTS ILLUSION

A. *Once the audience's perspective is pulled back, a slight shift of the puppeteer's frame-stage easily obscures elephants à la "thumb hides mountain" ploy.*

FIGURE 13: OBSCURING A FOE'S PERSPECTIVE

A. As the disguised shadowhander waves his fan, it blocks the sentry's view
à la "thumb hides mountain" ploy.

Optical Illusions

The eye sees not itself but a reflection, by some other things.

—Shakespeare
Julius Caesar

Gestalt psychology uses the term *prägnanz* to describe the tendency of the human brain to seek simplicity and balance. This takes the form of our grouping objects together that resemble each other and to our making "assumptions" about objects. For example, shown a series of dashes, we "see" a dotted line. Shown a series of unconnected points of light in the sky, we imagine figures and patterns and astrology is born. The best example of this tendency is a movie. A movie is merely a series of slightly different still pictures. Yet when these still pictures are flashed before our eyes at a set rate, the brain organizes the images into an optical illusion of a single moving picture.

Optical illusions can be created by simply adding perspective lines to make three same-size objects appear to be different in size (Figure 14).

At other times, same-size lines appear longer or shorter because the brain compares them to known phenomena. For example, the same-size lines in Figure 15 appear different because our brain associates them with the visual depth cues we use to identify structures.

More than just brain teasers, such optical illusions have practical application for many, from magicians to ruthless criminals.

Professional magicians routinely use the principles behind optical illusions on a grand scale when crafting their stage magic, using misleading visual cues to disguise cubbyholes big enough to hide an assistant or a tiger, and using visual distractions and designs to draw the audience's eyes away from where the real action is taking place (Poundstone 1993).

Like magicians, artists and movie FX specialists regularly use perspective to trick our eyes. So do crooks. Professional criminals (e.g., smugglers, burglars) know that when looking at

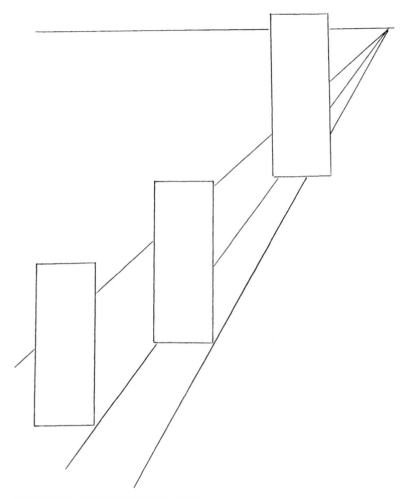

FIGURE 14: PERSPECTIVE LINES

several small boxes stacked haphazardly on top one another, our lazy minds see only that—small boxes stacked on top one another—never considering that the internal space created by linking those boxes together is more than big enough to hide a man (Figure 16).

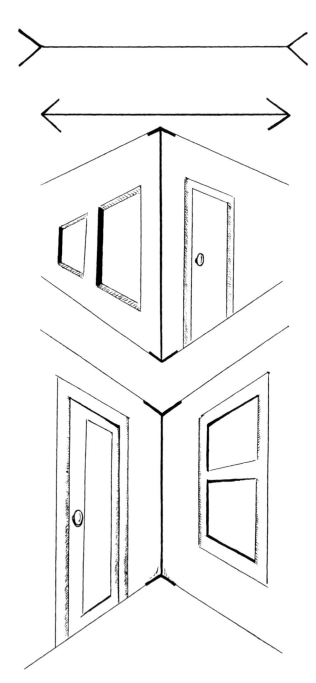

FIGURE 15: APPLICATION OF PERSPECTIVE LINES

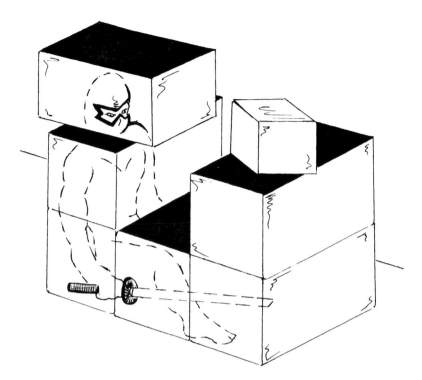

FIGURE 16: INTERNAL SPACE PLOY

The Trojans learned this principle the hard way. Mastery of this principle allowed ninja to hide themselves and their supplies and to penetrate and/or escape an enemy stronghold undetected.

Mastery of this principle also helps shadowhanders hide their weapons in plain sight. (See the section on kobudo-jutsu in Part II.)

Psychological Blind Spots

An open, relaxed hand can caress, grasp, and, when needed, close into a striking fist. Tightly clenched, a hand can only be used to strike. A tense mind is like a clenched fist: mental fears and tension prevent us from being fully functional.

—Dr. Haha Lung
Knights of Darkness, 1998

In the same way that certain physiolocical weaknesses in others can aid shadowhanders, so too can certain psycholocical factors contribute to the success of shadowhand. Various things, from strong emotions and laziness to an inability to see more than one use for an object to being too quick to "assume" and fill the blanks, can all make us—or our enemy—more vulnerable to attack. Life is a constant battle between reality and "really-like-it-to-be." All too often people see what they want to see because of personal likes and dislikes and/or because of social-religious prejudices instilled at an early age.

Our foes' prejudices and/or refusal to face reality can be turned to our advantage. An amusing yet apt observation of this principle comes to us in the 1973 movie *The Spook Who Sat by the Door* (based on the Sam Greenlee novel of the same name). Apart from being an insightful "training film" for urban guerrilla warfare, the movie sardonically observes that "a black man with a mop and bucket can go anywhere." The characters in the movie use this psychological blind spot in their foes to infiltrate heavily guarded installations and gather intelligence.

Ninja long ago recognized how seeding and encouraging such psychological blind spots can undermine an enemy's effectiveness.

Warning FLAGS

From the Chinese Taoists, moshuh nanren took the *wu hsing* ("five elements"), the theory that all reality is composed of five primordial elements that interact to either augment or cancel out the others.

Over the centuries, this theory has been applied to all aspects of life, including emotions and personalities. When this wu hsing philosophy washed ashore in Japan, the shinobi ninja further refined it and applied it specifically to overcoming their foes. Shinobi called this strategy *gojo-goyoku*, "the five weaknesses."

These five weaknesses are fear (*kyosha*), lust (*kisha*), anger (*dosha*), greed (*rakusha*) and sympathy (*aisha*). (NOTE: The first character of these five form the word "FLAGS," as in warning flags.)

We are all capable of expressing each of these emotions at any given time, in reaction to any given situation. However, we are

EMOTION	ANGER	LUST	SYMPATHY	GREED	FEAR
Japanese Name	*Ku*	*Ka*	*Chi*	*Fu*	*Sui*
Blind spot	Rage, Violence	Lust, Frustration	Pity, Helplessness	Laziness, Ruthlessness	Cowardice, Phobias
Your Attack Strategy	***Crush*** Overpower, Tempt Him to Act Rashly	***Pound*** Repeated Blows	***Cross*** Bypass, Distract	***Split*** Alienate, Divide His Attention	***Drill*** Plant Seeds of Doubt, Make Him Doubt His Senses

FIGURE 17: THE FIVE ELEMENTS BLIND SPOTS

also dominated by one of these "elements," and this makes up the bulk of our personality. Our personality, in turn, colors our reasoning and helps determine how accurately we "see" the world.

Knowing a foe's dominant emotion allows the ninja to either "feed" that failing, or else "starve" the foes of that emotion in order to make them more vulnerable.

Master Eastern strategists such as Sun Tzu, Tu Mu, and Miyamoto Musashi all preached the value of exploiting a foe's emotions, whether in conflicts involving armies of thousands, or during one-on-one combat.

If an enemy is reckless, he can easily be led to slaughter; fearful and hesitant, he can easily be captured. If he is quick to anger, you can easily make him a fool. If pretentious, upset him through slander and the planting of false gossip.
—Sun Tzu

Likewise, Sung dynasty strategist Chen Hao taught that the tactic of inciting blinding emotions such as lust and greed in an enemy must occupy an honored place in a general's bag of battlefield ploys.

For a full discussion on how to use *gojo-goyoku* to manipulate foes, see *Mindslayer! How to Control and Kill Others with Your Mind* (Lung and Prowant publication pending).

Object Fixedness

Pay attention now, or pay the doctor—or undertaker—later.
—Dirk Skinner
Street Ninja, 1998

Object fixedness is the human tendency to see only one use for an object. This failing prevents most people from "seeing" hundreds of potential defensive-offensive weapons available to them in any place at any given time (Omar 1993).

Taking advantage of this psychological blind spot in others allows shadowhanders to carry their weapons unnoticed. (See the section on kobudo-jutsu in Part II.)

The Straw Man

If these be true spies, which I wear in my head, here's a goodly sight.
—Shakespeare
The Tempest

Shinobi ninja used the term *amettori-no-jutsu* as a synonym for the art of deception and used it generically to describe various techniques of deceiving the human eye. *Amettori-no-jutsu* literally means "straw man" and derives from the ploy of setting up a scarecrow or similar shape that at first glance—especially at night—resembles an actual person. This ploy had numerous uses, from confusing an enemy as to the actual number of an attacking force to helping an individual ninja elude capture.

Professional night fighters often speak to novices of "getting your night eyes." This term refers not only to learning to see and move around in the dark but, more important, to cultivating the mind-set necessary for surviving at night.

In a similar fashion, to master the shadowhand you must get your "ninja eyes," that is, you must first learn to see beyond the "straw men" (obstacles seemingly impossible to pass) set up by your enemy—and by nature—and then learn how to effectively set up scarecrows of your own—physical and psychological—that will discourage, distract, and, when need be, destroy your foes.

This is accomplished by realizing that the same weaknesses that prevent us from "seeing" the world accurately also limit our enemies and that we can therefore use those weaknesses deliberately to keep enemy from seeing. Thus, those intent upon mastering the shadowhand must first learn to overcome their own blind spots before mastering the skill of exploiting those same blind spots in their foes.

Perception is strong, sight weak.

—Miyamoto Musashi

CHAPTER FIVE

The Quest for Invisibility

The quest for the secret of "true" invisibility has played an important role in the myths and methodology of many religious groups, secret societies, and killer cadres. As a result, tales testifying to the quest for the power of invisibility are found as far afield as the Australian Aborigines; among the ancient peoples of both North and South America; and in the East, in India and China, as well as among the shinobi ninja of Japan.

Down through the ages a variety of methods—from the use of magical garments to the muttering of sacred formulas—have been employed to produce invisibility. Some of these techniques were based on hard science, others on myth, pseudo-science, and superstition.

Some "invisibility" techniques are practical and physically

based (e.g., use of camouflage, understanding of chiaroscuro), while others are decidedly mystical and dependent on ritual practice and psychic processes.

All accounts of and speculations on the art of invisibility point to two distinct strategies.

The first requires physically changing objects (including yourself) to render them invisible.

The second calls for interfering with the perception of observers to prevent them from perceiving the (now) invisible object.

In the West, methods for accomplishing invisibility have generally involved acquiring a magical object, while in the East, mastering the art of invisibility usually requires learning a sacred word formula or mastering a "forbidden" yoga practice.

Even if we do not personally subscribe to the notion that actual invisibility is possible (even when produced by those methods that have behind them plausible scientific explanations), it is still important to study what others believe about invisibility. Understanding our enemies' personal beliefs and cultural superstitions (i.e., fears) about invisibility can give us valuable insight into defeating those enemies.

INVISIBILITY IN WESTERN TRADITION

In Greek mythology, the god Hermes gave Perseus a cap to wear that granted the hero invisibility. The Celtic hero Manannan Mac Lir possessed both a mantle and a helmet of invisibility. In the Northern European epic *Nibelungenlied* (first written down around 1200 CE), the hero, Siegfried, won a cloak of invisibility from the dwarf Alberich.

Ancient Scots Gaelic wizards and warriors had the *fith-fath* (pronounced "fee-fawh"), various charms that rendered them invisible and altered the wearers' appearance and form.

St. Patrick used a *fith-fath* to alter his form and that of monks traveling with him, to make himself and his fellow monks appear to be deer, thus allowing them to escape an evil king's henchmen.

In Switzerland, it is still widely held that if the amaranth (*Amaranthus*) flower is worn on Ascension Day it will render the wearer invisible. Amaranth—"the flower that never fades"—was also held sacred in Greco-Roman culture, where it was associated with immortality.

With the close of The Crusades, a multitude of secret societies and mystical enclaves sprang up throughout Europe. Many of these shadowy brotherhoods were believed to wield the power to "cloud" men's minds and become invisible.

From the 13th century on in Europe, numerous texts ranging from the factual to the fanciful claimed that various magicians and secret fraternities possessed the power of invisibility. Some of these writings were exposés warning of shadowy groups with questionable agendas, while other tracts were self-serving propaganda circulated by the groups themselves to enhance their own prestige.

The Shadow Knows!

A popular 1930s fictional character, The Shadow, was depicted as possessing the power to "cloud men's minds" and become invisible at will. It is curious that The Shadow creator Walter Gibson, himself a magician and dabbler in the occult, chose to use the phrase "cloud men's minds," since the use of mystical "clouds" to produce magical effects—especially invisibility—is a common occult theme running through Western accounts of invisibility.

From the Middle Ages on, several Western secret societies have claimed to possess the secret of turning invisible. The medieval Rosecrucian fraternity reportedly possessed the secret of invisibility, having inherited it from the Freemasons, who in turn were given (or had stolen!) the secret from fallen Knights Templar (themselves accused of having literally sold their souls to learn the secret from Satan himself or—worse yet—from the dreaded Muslim assassins (*hashishin*) of Syria (Lung 1997).

A paper reportedly written by Rosecrucians in the 15th century instructed initiates on "how to walk invisible among men." This Rosecrucian method claimed that invisibility could be produced through the use of "clouds" (i.e., bodies of "mist" conjured up to surround a person), effectively masking them from the sight of others (Higbee 1997: 35). Many claim that this secret practice is still taught today.

Several members of the 19th-century Spiritualist movement (beginning in the United States around 1848) claimed to have the power of invisibility. This Spiritualist method relied on separating the "astral body"—normally invisible to all but gifted observers—from the physical body.

During her intensive travels throughout the Far East, Madame H.P. Blavatsky (1831–1891) of the Theosophical Society (founded in 1875) reports having witnessed invisibility firsthand. After being initiated into the secret, Blavatsky claimed to have turned invisible on several occasions in full view of witnesses.

The Hermetic Order of the Golden Dawn (founded in 1888 in London) likewise left manuscripts describing the "Ritual of Invisibility" wherein initiates surrounded themselves with a mystical "shroud," described as looking like a "cloud." The Golden Dawn method is similar to, and perhaps derived from, earlier Rosecrucian and Masonic methods—not surprising, since a single thread of occultism binds all three.

(NOTE: During World War II, British intelligence maintained an "Occult Bureau," manned by such notables as Aldous Huxley and Ian Fleming [of James Bond fame]. At one point, Fleming reportedly attempted to employ the Golden Dawn's most notorious alumnus, Aleister Crowley, to interrogate the recently defected Rudolf Hess.) (Vankin 1992)

Reportedly, the "Occult Bureau" was also interested in picking Crowley's brain for any information he might have on the Golden Dawn's mastery of invisibility.)

Modern Accounts of Invisibility

Accounts of invisibility, some far-fetched, some credibly witnessed, have continued well into the 20th century. Western mystics still search for, teach, and practice (?) the art of invisibility.

How to render one's being invisible to other eyes, even although in a large crowd, through the formation of an enveloping astral shroud, is another branch of gray Magic existing between the Magic of Light and the dark.

—Israel Regardie
The Tree of Life, 1994

And what modern military strategist or night fighter wouldn't sell his soul for the real ability of invisibility?

Swedish mystic and playwright August Strindberg (1849–1912), a student of both alchemy and theosophy, traveled with a mysterious companion who reportedly possessed the ability to mask his aura to the point to where he couldn't be recognized (Wilson 1975: 31). Perhaps an example of the aforementioned amaranth use?

During World War II, Jewish psychic Wolf Messing was forced to flee from Poland to the Soviet Union after Hitler put a price on his head in response to Messing's prediction that Hitler would die "should the German dictator ever turn toward the East."

Intrigued by reports of Messing's psychic prowess, Soviet dictator Joseph Stalin wanted to use Messing's powers against his enemies but decided to test the psychic first. Stalin ordered Messing to prove his abilities to "cloud men's minds" by entering Stalin's country retreat without a pass. Soon after, while Stalin was working in his office, Messing coolly walked onto the grounds past dozens of heavily armed guards, straight into Stalin's study. Asked later how he accomplished this feat, Messing explained that by "mental suggestion" he had made Stalin's guards and servants think he was Lavrenty Beria, the much-feared head of the Soviet secret police. Though Messing looked nothing like Beria, the guards and servants were convinced he was (Wilson 1975: 19)

It might be argued that Messing's ability to disguise himself, as well as Strindberg's companion's ability to "mask his aura," were more "shape-shifting" than true "invisibility." Shape-shifting, the ability to literally alter one's form, has been the inspiration for yet another quest—by everyone from sundry magicians to warrior groups (ranging from the thugee and ninja of the East to the berserkers and wolfshirts of medieval Northern Europe).

Like accounts of invisibility, many of the tales of heroes and mysterious brotherhoods possessing the power to alter their shape at will are based on physical legerdemain.

Not surprisingly, individuals and cadres to whom such powers—from shape-shifting to invisibility—are attributed seldom go out of their way to convince others, especially superstitious enemies, that they do not possess such magical powers.

Respected researcher Donna Higbee has recorded numerous modern accounts of what she refers to as "human spontaneous involuntary invisibility" (HSII), instances where ordinary people unintentionally become invisible. Higbee records one woman's experiences at a police station where, surrounded by professionally trained observers, the woman nonetheless remained invisible.

Higbee's cases of HSII share certain similarities. First, the invisible person is still physically present but is unable to be seen or heard by others. Second, from the POV of the invisible person, the world still looks normal; often the invisible person has no idea that he or she cannot be seen or heard by others (Higbee 1997: 34).

INVISIBILITY IN EASTERN TRADITION

As in the West, the quest for true invisibility was manifested in various forms and traditions in several schools and sects of the Far East with, surprisingly, quite a bit of interchange of ideas taking place between these various traditions and groups.

The shinobi ninja art of invisibility, for example, began in ancient India, climbed the Himalayas to Tibet, and traveled the length of China before setting sail for Japan.

Indian Invisibility Techniques
No one knows for sure how far back the quest for the secret of invisibility goes in ancient India. We do know that the secret of invisibility was actively sought and, if accounts widely

believed in are to be believed, practiced by various sects in India from ancient times up through the 19th and 20th (?) centuries.

We know that Indo-European beliefs in invisibility were brought into the Indus Valley with the Aryan invaders, circa 2500–1500 BCE (Before Common Era) (Higbee 1997: 34).

Other Indo-European groups also maintained traditions of invisibility. The Hittites, rulers of an empire stretching across the Middle East and Turkey (circa 1900–1200 BCE), had many gods, each of which granted special powers to their worshippers. These included a god who could make Hittite warriors invisible to their enemies.

Ancient rituals and techniques, some describing techniques of invisibility, are described in the Hindu Vedic ("knowledge") texts, which were written down about 1400–1000 BCE (Higbee 1997).

In the *Kama Sutra of Vatsyayana*, composed between the 1st and 4th centuries CE and introduced to the West by Sir Richard Burton in 1883, there is a recipe by which a man can render himself invisible:

> The heart of an ichneumon, the fruit of the long gourd (*Tumbi*), and the eyes of a serpent should all be burnt without letting out the smoke, the ashes should then be ground and mixed in equal quantities with water. By putting this mixture upon the eyes a man can go about unseen. Other means of invisibility are prescribed by Duyana Brahmans and Jogashiras.[1]

In his 3rd century *Yoga Sutra*, Hindu Master Pantaniali also describes how human invisibility is possible. According to Pantanjali, a yogi gathers energy through *samyama* ("perfected ritual and discipline") such as concentration and meditation. A natural outgrowth of such practice is the development of fantastic powers (*siddhas*), including the power of invisibility.

In *Yoga Sutra* verse 21, Pantajali outlines the specific process by which invisibility occurs: "By performing perfect practice (*samyama*), we suspend the receptive power of sight (*rupa-tanamatra*), the connection between the eye of the observer and the light reflecting off the body of the observed is broken and the body of the observed becomes invisible."

Believe it or not, Pantanjali's method has a solid basis in modern science. An object (e.g., the human body) is seen ("becomes visible") when light reflecting off it is registered by the eye of the perceiver. If that light is not reflected, or if contact between the eye of the observer and the light reflecting off the object (e.g., your body) can be distorted or blocked, your body will be "invisible" to the observer.

LIGHT FROM OBJECT————BLOCKED————"INVISIBLE"

Through Pantanjali's "perfect practice" (e.g., meditation, ritual chanting) a yogaman literally changes the "vibration" of his body to the point to where his body absorbs rather than reflects light wavelengths. Since no light is reflected off the object, no reflected light is seen and the yogaman remains invisible to the human eye.

Note that this is the same principle behind modern "stealth" technology. Radar bounces off objects, and the returning radar signal tells the radar screen that something is there. Modern stealth craft are designed to absorb (or deflect) radar signals. Since the radar signals do not return to their point of origin, the craft remains "invisible" to radar.

The *Anahata Chakra*

In yogic tradition, invisibility is controlled by the 4th (*anahata*) *chakra*. (*Chakras* are "power centers" scattered throughout the body, believed to connect the physical body with a spiritual "aura" that surrounds the human body.) Yogamen who master this *chakra* (situated near the heart) gain a host of powers, including the ability to make themselves invisible. In yogic lore, meditation focusing on this *anahata chakra* helps us balance our physical and emotional energies.

All perception is based on contrast. Therefore, if we could remain perfectly "balanced" physically and emotionally—without perceivable vibrations fluctuating one way or the other—it would be impossible for another person to perceive us since we would be in perfect synch—balanced—with any background, hence invisible.

According to yogic masters, meditation using the mantra-chant assigned to the anahata chakra "yam" helps us attain this perfectly balanced—and invisible!—state.

The *Mahashunya*

Practical application of Indian invisibility technique was exhibited by the thugee cultists who terrorized India from ancient times up through the mid-19th century (Lung 1995).

Beyond the use of conventional secrecy and stealth movement demanded of their dark calling, these killers for the goddess Kali were widely rumored—a rumor never discouraged by thuggee themselves—to have had at their disposal an ancient and mystical method of invisible movement known as *mahashunya*, "the great void of silence."

When employing *mahashunya*, thuggee adepts physically slipped into a *mahashunya* "doorway" no one else could see, disappearing from human sight, only to step "out" of a similar "doorway" and reappear, often miles from their original "entry" point.

To accomplish this effect, thuggee used a variation of the anahata chakra chant "yam" to change their overall mental and physical vibration, allowing them to perceive where mahashunya "doorways" were to be found. (NOTE: Some have suggested that accounts of the original "Indian rope trick" [where a fakir or his assistant disappears atop a rope hung on nothing] was based on this same mahashunya technique . . . or at least on its legend.) Modern researchers have speculated that mahashunya may be terrestrial versions of "wormholes," space anomalies that, hypothetically, would allow a spacecraft to enter at one point in the galaxy and exit at a second point millions of light - years away in distant space.

It has even been proposed that this mahashunya/wormhole phenomenon may be behind an unexplained incident known to popular folklore as "the Philadelphia experiment." Reportedly, in October 1943, the naval ship USS *Eldridge* simply vanished with its crew from a heavily guarded Philadelphia naval yard. From what has been pieced together (50 years later, with much about the incident still "classified"), the ship "dematerialized" following a series of experiments attempting to use "magnetic manipulations" to make a ship "invisible" to radar. One theory is that one or a combination of these experiments accidently projected the ship and crew into another "dimension" after inadvertently tapping into mahashunya. A simpler explanation is that the magnetic experiments somehow changed the vibrations of the ship (and crew), making the vessel vibrate at a faster rate of speed so that it was "invisible" to the human eye.

By the way, the Indian thuggee provide an interesting link between secret societies and mystical schools of East and West. The thuggee were heavily infiltrated by the Persian branch of the *hashishin* (assassins) who, in turn, influenced the mythology and methods of several European secret societies via the equally mysterious Knights Templar (Lung 1995: 1997).

SHINOBI NINJA INVISIBILITY

In Japan there is the tale of the mischievous boy who tricks a *tengu* (lit. long-nose) demon, into trading away his "cloak of leaves" that granted the wearer invisibility.

The boy predictably used his newfound invisibility to play spiteful tricks on people until the *tengu* retrieved his cloak (via the *tengu's* innate ability to see the boy even when the boy was invisible).

Many in Japan believe this cautionary tale was inspired by the true life adventures of 12th-century samurai hero Yoshitsune, who reportedly hid out among the shinobi-ninja clans while plotting the overthrow of his evil brother, the shogun.

That the shinobi ninja possessed the power of invisibility was universally believed. From whom—and how—they acquired this power is the subject of speculation and dispute. We know shinobi *jonin* (lit. leaders) sent spies abroad to glean both exoteric and esoteric secrets from cults and cadre such as the thugee of India, the sdop sdop warrior-monks of Tibet, and the moshu nanren ninja of China. Not the least of the secrets brought back by these agents were methods for creating true invisibility.

* * * * *

Noteworthy is the widespread belief that ninja were capable of detaching their bodily shadow. This shadow body (some researchers equate it with the "astral body") had the ability to move about undetected, entering any shadow anywhere and exiting a similar shadow anywhere else in the world, traveling great distances and penetrating any enemy stronghold effortlessly.

This technique calls to mind the mahashunya traveling of Indian thugee adepts.

* * * * *

Through the ages, various Eastern martial arts masters have been credited with possessing the power of invisibility. In modern times, Ueshiba Morehei, founder of aikido, was witnessed on several occasions to simply vanish from sight, only to reappear later at another location.

EXPLANATIONS FOR INVISIBILITY

Numerous theories have been given to explain how physical invisibility might actually occur. These explanations range from descriptions of how physical camouflage works to psychic and scientific explanations—both of which hold out the possibility for "true" invisibility.

Physical Explanations

The purely physical means of interrupting another's perception and making oneself "invisible" is called camouflage (from the French, literally "smoke in the eyes"). Camouflage is a vital survival skill for any killer cadre involved in skulduggery, ninja not excluded. For the constantly besieged shinobi clans, mastering camouflage involved such things as remaining perfectly still in order to evade searchers; learning to disguise entrances to a home's escape tunnel; and mastering the art of disguising shape, shadow, and movement in order to penetrate an enemy citadel.

Mastering camouflage begins with understanding how an eye sees and then preventing it from doing so. Recall that the human eye first sees movement, then captures silhouette (outline, shape), and finally discerns color.

Remaining completely still defeats perception of movement.

Disguising shape and silhouette and changing color help objects (including ourselves) better blend into the background, rendering us "invisible" to observers (Lung 1998).

Scientific Explanations

In H.G. Wells's 1897 novel *The Invisible Man*, a young scientist named Griffin, assisted by a tramp named Marvel, spends three years studying "reflections of light," theorizing that a man could become invisible if his cells were made "transparent."

Having succeeded in making himself invisible but unable to reverse the process, Griffin is eventually driven mad. Once he's killed by authorities, his body reappears.

Reminiscent of standard yogic practice, Griffin had to fast from eating while invisible, since swallowed food would remain visible in his stomach. (NOTE: This blend of science and mysticism mirrors Wells's own interests in life.)

Although *The Invisible Man* remains fiction, the facts of known science point to the possibility that physical invisibility can indeed be achieved. That free electrons absorb light is a scientific principle. Certain "occult" rituals seem to naturally "attract" free electrons, thus opening the possibility for producing invisibility. A cloud of free electrons absorbs all light entering it and does not reflect or refract light waves. In addition, light waves are not able to pass through a human body. Consequently, an observer looking at a person surrounded by such a cloud of free electrons will see nothing there. Light is necessary for human sight; thus when there are no reflected light waves bouncing off a person and hitting the observer's eye, the observed person remains invisible to the observer (Higbee 1997: 35).

The Psychic Explanation

According to Gregory Little in his *People of the Web*, other levels of existence are all around us but, because these other "dimensions" operate at a "higher" vibration rate, they remain invisible to normal perception. "Raising" our own vibration rate allows us to perceive these "higher" realms of existence. However, "raising" our bodily vibration can inadvertently make us "invisible" to those individuals still vibrating in synch with the mundane world.

(NOTE: Belief in one or more versions of this psychic theory for invisibility and other ESP phenomena helps explain why many killer cadres, such as the thugee, the hashishin, and the ninja, insist that trainees study metaphysics to augment their purely physical skills.)

INVISIBILITY VERSUS SHADOWHAND

It is no secret that mastering the art of invisibility, whether the purely physical camouflage variety, or some "mystical" version, gave the ninja a distinct advantage over their foes. Even the superstitious belief by foes that ninja possessed such a secret gave the ninja a decided advantage. Thus the saying, "Reputation spills less blood."

Taisavaki shadowhand techniques fall somewhere in between the two extremes of mystical belief in the power of a man to turn himself invisible and the practical study of how to mislead an enemy's eye into seeing incorrectly or not at all. While based on sound physical principles of movement, shadowhand strategy and tactics work only if we take the time to first master the psychology of seeing (review Chapter 4: The Basics of Seeing).

An understanding of both human physiology and psychology worked hand in hand to allow the ninja to miraculously "appear" out of nowhere, materializing in front of or behind a foe, and strike that foe with one or more "invisible" blows before "disappearing" from the enemy's sight altogether.

Mastery of both physical and psychological shadowhand strategies and tactics will allow us to do the same.

ENDNOTE

1. Ichneumon refers to either a mongoose or a fly. In this instance one assumes it is the former. "Duyana Brahmans" and "Jogashiras" refer to specific schools of thought.

PART 2

Application:
Mastering the Shadowhand

Once we understand how the eye gets its information, it is a simple matter to confuse an enemy's eye into misinterpreting incoming information.

—Dr. Haha Lung
Knights of Darkness, 1998

Having come to appreciate the context in which shadow-hand strategy and technique was conceived, was finely honed, and has been used in actual kill-or-be-killed struggles through the ages, we can now turn our study to acquiring and correctly applying those strategies and techniques of the shadowhand that will vouchsafe our survival while guaranteeing the downfall of our foes.

CHAPTER SIX

The Strategy of the Shadowhand

According to Sun Tzu, there are two types of "force" a general has at his disposal: *cheng* ("direct force") and *ch'i* ("indirect force"). These two are sometimes referred to respectively as "normal" (i.e., covert, easily seen) and "extraordinary" (i.e., misleading and covert).

As military forces go, *cheng* manifests itself as conventional troops, while *chi* amounts to special forces and irregulars, such as guerrilla fighters.

In larger field operations, *cheng* strategy is the overt movement of troops and equipment that is easily seen (or is allowed to be "discovered") by an enemy. Such open operations allow a general to divert his enemy's attention while hiding his true intention.

For example, a loud and raucous massing of conventional army units directly across from enemy lines or outside an enemy's stronghold is used to "fix" the enemy's attention, drawing that attention away from the actual target.

Once the enemy's attention is fixed on your *cheng* force, your *chi* forces attack when and where their blows are not anticipated. In other words, my direct (*cheng*) assault on your front gate covers my special forces (*ch'i*) slipping over your stronghold's back wall.

Says Sun Tzu, "While *cheng* engages, *ch'i* wins."

When this principle of *cheng/ch'i* is applied to personal combat, it forms the basis for the shadowhand. For example, an obvious *cheng* movement outward draws an opponent's attention outward, allowing you to suddenly strike inward with an oblique and decisive *ch'i* technique (see Figure 3).

This interplay of *cheng* and *ch'i* allows you to accomplish the two main objectives of the shadowhand: disguising your intention while diverting your enemy's attention.

DISGUISING INTENTION

It is easier to bring down a foe when he doesn't yet suspect you are moving against him. Unfortunately, it's all too common to inadvertently expose your intention and give away your plan of attack by your attitude during your approach or during the initial seconds of your attack against a foe. In effect, you "telegraph" your intention.

According to Sun Tzu, deception (i.e., cheng and ch'i working in concert) is the essence of all warfare. Thus, deception—disguising one's intention when moving against a foe—is a vital skill for the shadowhander to master. To accomplish this, the shadowhander learns the art of disguising three things: attitude, approach to an enemy, and then the actual attack.

Attitude

Novice beekeepers are taught that in order to avoid being stung, in order to remain calm around a swarm of bees, they should picture a hexagon—the shape of a honeycomb—in their minds. According to knowledgeable apiculturists, their visualizing this hexagon calms the bees.

Regardless of whether this kind of visualization actually has an effect on the bees themselves, it does help calm the novice beekeeper (if only by taking his or her mind off being stung). A calmer, less clumsy, less fearful beekeeper incites the bees less.

In the same way, your attitude, your mind-set, as you approach a foe (whether one who knows you are his enemy or one who doesn't have a clue that he has been targeted) is vitally important.

In a face-to-face confrontation, projecting a confident attitude can unnerve even the most cocksure of foes. Street punks routinely bypass those who walk with a confident, self-assured step, head up and alert, in favor of mugging those who shuffle along fearfully, heads down, oblivious to their surroundings (Skinner 1995).

Other times, it's necessary to get close enough to an enemy to strike before he is aware of being targeted. Unfortunately, we all too often give off subtle and subconscious signals that inadvertently alert a foe to our intention.

Masking Your *Wa*

Through meditation and mastery of body language, ninja shadowhanders learned to disguise their intention to do others harm. This allowed them to draw close enough to their victims to deliver the coup de grace. Ninja refer to this as masking their *wa*. *Wa* can be translated as "presence," "aura," or "intent".

Some adept and attuned martial arts masters can "read" other people's *wa* and determine as they approach whether they have "evil intentions" in their heart. Other times, these masters can "sense" another's intention just as the person prepares to strike a treacherous blow. Some possess this ability from birth; the rest of us have to work at it. (See Uncommon "Sense" in Chapter 4.)

The ability to "mask the *wa*" allows shadowhanders to disguise any telling body tension and/or revealing emotion (e.g., overt hate for an enemy, excitement, fear) that their targeted foe might pick up on—either consciously or subconsciously.

English-speaking adherents of the shadowhand often euphemistically refer to masking the *wa* as "learning to hide the beast."

To mask your *wa,* visualize the end result. What this means is not allowing yourself to "awful-ize" on all the possible things that can go wrong. Rather, "see" yourself after the fact—once you have successfully approached a foe without alerting him; once you have struck the telling shadowhand blow; once you have made good your egress.

Now, as you draw near your target, keep this end-result image fixed in your mind. (NOTE: This is similar to the rule of never looking directly at an enemy sentry as you "approach him for removal" (see Figure 9).

Approach

It is important to learn to disguise your body language when approaching a foe face to face for open combat, especially when trying to get near a foe without alerting that foe as to your intention to inflict bodily harm (e.g., when approaching an enemy while in disguise).

The ability to disguise one's walk and demeanor—to convincingly appear as an aged monk, a crippled beggar, a young maiden—was a vital skill taught in the ninja's sixth training hall, the art of disguise. (See The Nine Training Halls of Ninjutsu, Chapter 2.)

Ninja also learned to disguise their overall direction of movement when moving against an enemy—whether during field operations or when locked in singular hand-to-hand combat.

Recall that when approaching an enemy sentry from behind, ninja sappers always used a zigzag approach and were always careful to come in under a sentry's LOS (see Figure 9).

Likewise, when engaged in one-on-one combat, ninja fighters mastered the art of dropping inside and under an attacker's LOS in order to come up inside an opponent's attack or even behind the opponent's back, where the finishing shadowhand blow could be struck. (See section below on *ukemi*/methods of movement.)

Attack!

When attacking enemies, ninja rarely took a straight-in, linear approach. Rather, they attacked at an oblique angle designed to make their enemies think they were fleeing—before suddenly turning back inward to attack!

In other situations, the ninja purposely feigned an obvious (cheng) strike to one body target in order to set up his actual (ch'i) strike to another body target. Specialized methods of movement used to accomplish this are known as *ukemi*.

Ukemi (Methods of Movement)

The specialized methods of movement, or *ukemi*, ninja used to disguise their movements were of two types: inside movement and outside movement. Inside movements allowed the ninja to move safely into the attack zone, close enough to where he could strike down a foe, preferably without being hit![1] Outside movements allowed the ninja to sidestep and shift out of the way of a foe's attack. Inside movements and outside movements were then paired with the 10 directions of movement. These 10 directions of movement used during shadowhand combat consist of the eight points on a compass (north, south, east, west, northeast southeast, southwest, and northwest), "up," and "down." (See Figure 18.)

Mastery of these simple 10 directions of movement allows the student to perform more complex (more effective) methods of movement.

To help students visualize the methods/directions of movement, shadowhand instructors use a numbered nine-sectioned diamond shape consisting of nine approximately 1-foot squares drawn on the dojo floor.

To use this diamond, the student identifies his feet as left (L) and right (R), followed by the particular square that foot is touching. For example, beginning with his feet on square 1 (L1 and R1, facing north), to step straight forward, the student steps R1 to R5, then moves L1 to L9. Standing on square 9 (L9 and R9) facing north, to move backward (south) in a straight line, he steps L9 to L5 and then R9 to R1.

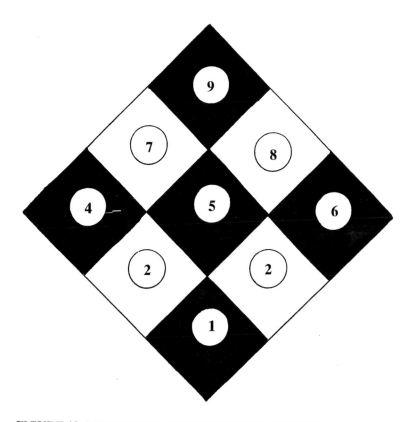

FIGURE 18: DIRECTIONS-OF-MOVEMENT DIAMOND

The following nine *ukemi* techniques form the basis for the shadowhander's methods of movement.

Forward Diagonal Step

To avoid a foe's attack along a straight 9-5-1 line of attack (e.g., a straight right-leading-hand punch), the shadowhander responds by stepping L1 to L4. Faced with a left leading-hand punch, you step R1 to R6. This diagonal step moves you out of your foe's straight LOS and to the outside of his attacking arm. This forces his eyes to follow you while he attempts to check his forward momentum and reestablish his attack (Figure 19).

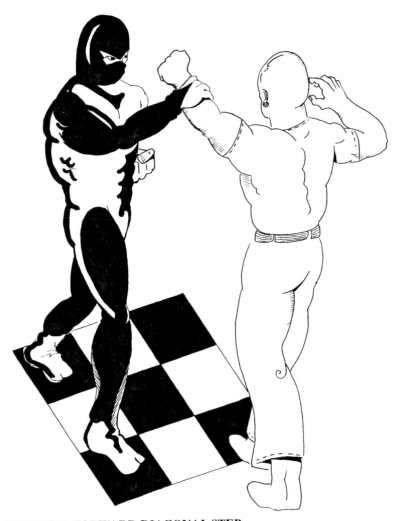

FIGURE 19: FORWARD DIAGONAL STEP

Half-Moon Step

When moving forward in what appears to be a straight 1-5-9 line, employ the half-moon step, which shifts your weight out and then inward as your leading leg whips first in (toward the other leg) and then back out. This semicircular pattern of stepping allows the shadowhander to avoid (slip) an opponent's punch before turning back in for a counterattack. (See Figure 20.)

The formula for the half-moon step is L1 to L4, R1 to R9. Note, however, that as the right foot moves forward, it first goes toward the left foot (L4) before landing on square 9.

This movement carries your weight first left, then back in right for your counterattack.

The foot placement of half-moon stepping automatically places your foot down behind an opponent's leading leg in ideal position for a "kickback sweep." (See the section below on tai-jutsu/unarmed combat.)

To move to the rear, simply reverse your half-moon movements.

Over-the-Fence Pivot

Standing on L1–R1 (facing east), pick up R1 and, pivoting on your left foot west, place R1 down on square 5 into a horse stance, now facing west (L1–R5).

Perform a left over-the-fence by picking up L1, pivoting on your right foot, and placing L1 down on square 9.

(NOTE: As shown in Figure 21, you raise your foot to pivot and bring it up to knee level (as if stepping over a small fence, hence the name).

This over-the-fence pivot has many applications, from the defensive deflection of a foe's attack to an offensive sweep and/or spinning-in foot strike. (See the sections on daikentai-jutsu and jutaijutsu in Chapter 7.)

Switch-Back Pivot

This is similar to the over-the-fence pivot, except that it uses a diagonal line of movement.

Having performed a half-moon step (L1 to L4, then R1 to R9, facing north), pick up your L4 foot and put it down at L6, pivoting on your right foot (R9) as you do. As you pivot, raise your left foot approximately six inches to one foot off the floor (Figure 22).

FIGURE 20: HALF-MOON STEP

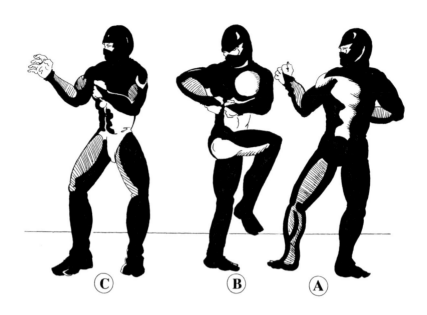

FIGURE 21: OVER-THE-FENCE PIVOT
A. *Beginning in a horse stance,*
B. *raise your right rear leg and pivot on your left leading leg.*
C. *Place your right (now leading) foot down forward. The whole movement should resemble having stepped over a short obstacle (e.g., small fence, log).*

Chinese Shift

The Chinese shift step isn't actually a step per se; rather, it is a shifting of your weight that allows you to slip an attacker's punch. Rather than moving the feet, you turn the foot closest the attacker up on its heel, shifting your weight into a back stance balanced on your back foot (Figure 23).

Horse-Stance Shift

Aligned with an attacking foe (see Figure 6), spin away from the attacker's punch or kick by picking up your leading foot and placing it down to the rear. Example: beginning with L5–RS (facing north), R5 moves to R1 (facing east). (See Figure 24.)

This shift can also be used offensively, into an opponent, in order to deliver a kick (see the section on daikentaijutsu).

FIGURE 22: SWITCH-BACK PIVOT

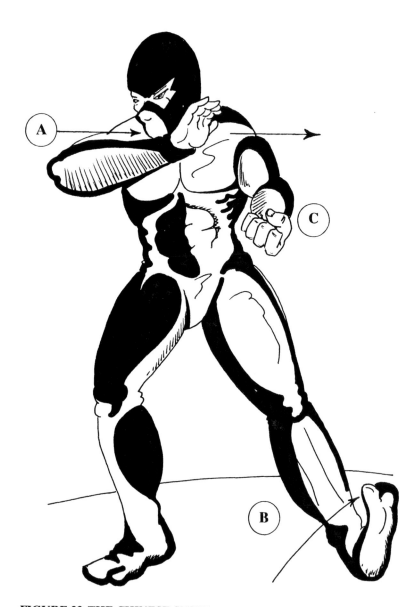

FIGURE 23: THE CHINESE SHIFT

A. *Employing a cross-body block to push aside an attacking hand,*

B. *simultaneously shift your weight to your rear foot while turning your lead foot onto its heel.*

C. *This places you out of the "line of fire" and in perfect position to counter-strike.*

FIGURE 24: HORSE-STANCE SHIFT

The Duck

Positioned at Ll–R1 (facing north), respond to a right-arm or high-level leg attack by squatting down while simultaneously stepping L1 to L4, coming up out of your squat after you pass under the attacking limb.

Your ducking under your opponent's attacking limb skews his straight LOS, forcing his eyes to try to follow your movement. As you "reappear" on the outside of his line of attack, your foe's extended attacking limb partially obscures his vision, helping to disguise your shadowhand counterstrike (Figure 25).

When ducking under the attacking limb, never bend over forward, exposing your neck and spine to attack. Instead, squat onto your knees, compressing the springs in your legs. This gives you explosive power when coming up out of your squat for your counterattack.

Chinese Squat

An effective variation of the duck is the Chinese squat (Figure 26). To perform the Chinese squat while standing at Ll–R1 (facing east), R1 passes behind L1 to square 5. As R1 steps onto square 5, your weight automatically lowers and you drop under your opponent's direct LOS.

The Chinese squat can be used both offensively (moving forward, striking) and defensively (performing the same stepping pattern in reverse, blocking or counterstriking).

The Chinese squat has a multitude of defensive and offensive uses. (See the sections on daikentaijutsu and jutaijutsu in Chapter 7.)

FIGURE 26: THE CHINESE SQUAT

(NOTE: Versions of the Chinese squat that do not squat as low are sometimes referred to as the "cross-over step."

Arch Escape

Whereas the duck takes advantage of an opening caused by an enemy's attack, the arch escape technique makes an opening through coordination of an offensive stepping pattern and a defensive rising block.

Standing Ll–R1 (facing north), respond to the enemy's right leading punch with a sweeping left high-rising block. As your rising arm blocks the attacker's arm, it creates an "arch."

Simultaneously with successfully blocking the attacking arm, your left foot turns in place and you move forward diagonally R1 to R4, passing under the "arch" made by your blocking arm and the arm of your attacker.

Your escaping through this arch places you in a perfect position to counterattack with various striking, sweeping, and grappling techniques. (See Figure 27.)

Arches are created anytime an enemy swings in his arm, whether armed or unarmed, and/or are when he throws any inward-swinging arching kick (e.g., a roundhouse or a crescent-type kick).

Shadowhanders train so that anytime such an arch presents itself, they will dash through it like a like a man escaping from a burning house.

An escaping ninja, having passed through a doorway, would discourage pursuit by stringing a tripwire or other booby trap across the doorway he'd just escaped through. At other times, a closely pursued ninja would quickly turn back to wait just outside the archway with sword, bow, or other weapon at the ready to cut down any pursuers.

Often ninja worked in teams, with one or more *genin* (operative) assigned to guard the team's egress by cutting down and otherwise discouraging any pursuers through the laying of booby traps (e.g., tripwires, seeding caltrops).

So, too, having passed through the arch created by his successfully blocking his foe's punching or high-kicking attack, the shadowhander is then in perfect position to pivot back into his attack-

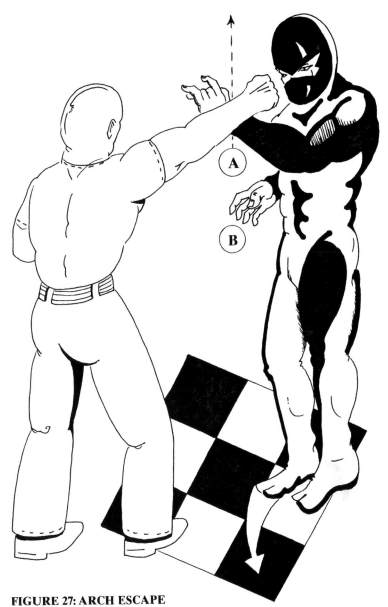

FIGURE 27: ARCH ESCAPE

A As your foe attacks, block his attacking arm out and up, creating an
   "arch." Simultaneously with creating this arch, step diagonally under it,
   away from your foe's line of attack.

B As you slip through the arch, attack into your foe's "centerline" with your
   ʒe arm.

er with numerous devastating counterattacks. (See the daikentai-jutsu, jutaijutsu, and kobudo-jutsu sections in Chapter 7.)

MISDIRECTING ATTENTION

Alarm him to the front to surprise him to the rear. Create uproar in the east to strike in the west.

—Chang Yu,
Sung dynasty strategist

When the shadowhander cannot completely disguise his intention to strike a foe, or when he needs to distract a foe's attention as part of the overall attack plan the shadowhander can often utilize the simplest of techniques, including making small noises and the classic pebble over the shoulder, the "oldest trick in the book."

Remember: tricks well mastered are called "techniques;" techniques half-learned are merely tricks. Thus, in the hands of a shadowhander the simple slight-of-hand trick of palming a coin (see Figure 2) can be used to steal a vital key, replacing it with a phony key, or to shift a small weapon (e.g., *shuriken* throwing star, razor blade) from one hand to the other.

On a bigger scale, this same trick (technique) can be used to make a pursuing enemy think the shadowhander has zigged when actually he's zagged.

(NOTE: Even when such a simple trick graduates to become a deadly technique, it still must be adapted to fit circumstances. For example, the technique described in Figure 28 might work well in an urban setting, but it will need to be modified for use in a rural setting.)

And, as described in Part I, shadowhanders use a multitude of camouflage tactics, as well as techniques designed to disguise shape, silhouette, and color, all in an effort to disguise their intention and distract a foe's attention (Figure 29).

ENDNOTE

1. Some martial arts schools preach the importance of a student being able to "take one to get one" (i.e., to toughen the body in expectation of getting hit, to be able

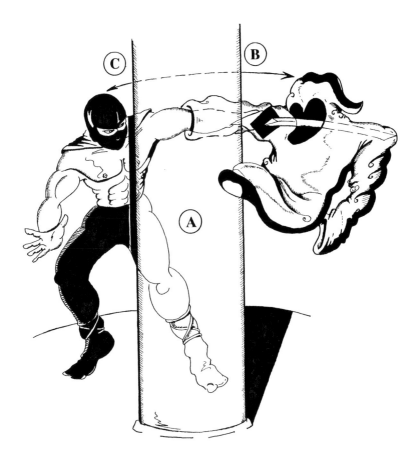

FIGURE 28: MISDIRECTING MOVEMENT

A. *Temporarily obscured from sight behind an obstacle (in this case, a pillar),*

B. *the shadowhander dodges to the right,*

C. *misdirecting his foe's attention leftward by tossing his shirt (or other distracting object) to the left.*

to survive a foe's blows while maneuvering yourself into position to deliver blows of your own). While the realities of combat dictate that you cannot always escape unscathed, the shadowhand way is to spend more time training not to get hit, rather than hoping to survive a hit.

On the flipside, shadowhanders hope that their foes study at this "take one to get one" school, since shadowhanders subscribe to the ancient Japanese martial arts ideal *"ikken hisatsu,"* "to kill with one blow."

In other words, if this *ikken hisatsu* blow is the one you are required to "take" in order to "get one" of your own, you could end up disappointed—or dead!

FIGURE 29: DISGUISING MOVEMENT/DIRECTION

A *Having secured his shirt to a bent-back branch, the shadowhander releases the branch, which snaps forward from the left, startling his foe.*

B. *Simultaneously, the shadowhander attacks (or escapes) by dodging to the right.*

C. *The effectiveness of the whipping branch can be augmented by purposely sharpening protruding smaller limbs.*
   (NOTE: This same ploy can be set up as a booby trap triggered by a tripwire.)

CHAPTER SEVEN

Techniques of the Shadowhand

Plan no useless move. Take no step in vain.

—Ch'en Hao
Sung dynasty

Shadowhanders use the Japanese term *taijutsu* ("skill with the body") as a catchall for personal combat, as well as a synonym for martial arts.

Taijutsu comprises the *ukemi* specialized methods of movement already described, as well as daikentaijutsu (striking skills such as kicks and punches), jutaijutsu (grappling skills), and kobudo-jutsu (weapons use).

These disciplines are not exclusive; instead they overlap, complement, and work in concert with one another. For example, the same foot movements and arm positions used to set up a telling unarmed blow are also used when wielding a weapon.

DAIKENTAIJUTSU (STRIKING)

Skirt an enemy's defenses. Appear where he least expects you; slip in where he is empty; strike where he is void.

—Ts'ao Ts'ao
155–220 C.E.

Almost any part of the human body can be used as an offensive striking weapon. Of course, some body parts are naturally more effective bludgeons than others. Our hands and feet are our foremost striking weapons. However, elbows, knees, wrists, head, shoulders, and hips can also be used.

To ensure that they have an endless arsenal of at-the-ready striking weapons, shadowhanders use the collapsing principle.

The Collapsing Principle

The shadowhand collapsing principle employs a succession of rapid-fire strikes, one strike following immediately upon the preceding one without the shadowhander's having to withdraw and rechamber his striking hands and feet. For example, after striking with a punch, rather than withdraw his hand (as would a Western boxer), the shadowhander continues his forward momentum by "collapsing" into an elbow strike and then, if necessary, a forceful blow with his shoulder designed to further unbalance his foe.

This collapsing principle strategy is similar to that used in drunken-style kung-fu, wherein an adept feigns intoxication to get a foe to drop his guard. The "drunken" adept then "staggers and stumbles," "falls," and/or rolls into his foe, in the process pummeling that foe with a flurry of "accidental" rapid-fire blows (Figure 30).

Striking with the Hands

With the possible exception of the boxer's close-in uppercut, the straight-in, aligned (see Figure 6) punches indicative of Western boxing are easily spotted and followed by the human eye.

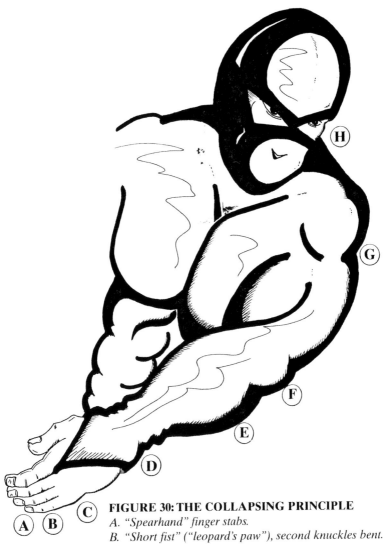

FIGURE 30: THE COLLAPSING PRINCIPLE

A. *"Spearhand" finger stabs.*

B. *"Short fist" ("leopard's paw"), second knuckles bent.*

C. *Traditional closed-fist strikes.*

D. *"Turtle's head" wrist strike (see Figure 43).*

E. *Forearm strike (see Figure 44) .*

F. *"Short wing" elbow strikes (see Figures 45 through 48)*

G. *Shoulder strike*

H. *Head butt (See Figure 49)*

Eastern martial arts on the other hand, and especially Chinese kung-fu styles, use deceptive movements and oblique strikes that are not so easily detected and/or followed by the eye (see Figure 3).

This kind of deceptive moving and striking is also the hallmark of the shadowhand.

Shadowhand techniques are designed to distract a foe's sight up or down and/or otherwise obscure his view, making that foe's attack and/or his defense against your counterattack all the more difficult.

Striking Inside

Using the forward diagonal step (Figure 19) places you outside your foe's extended attacking hand. In this position, his extended arm partially obscures his view, allowing you to attack back inside with a shadowhand strike (Figure 31).

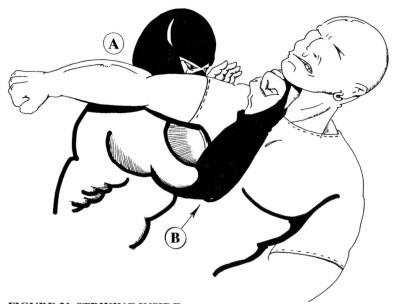

FIGURE 31: STRIKING INSIDE
A. *Having slipped to the outside of your foe's leading punch using either a forward diagonal step (Figure 19) or the duck (Figure 25),*
B. *counterstrike up and into your foe's "centerline" (groin, solar plexus, throat, chin, face).*

The Rising Sun

A variation of this diagonal step/uppercut technique, known as the rising sun, employs the shadowhand collapsing principle.

Having performed the forward diagonal step, strike upward inside your foe's attacking arm with a palm strike to his chin. As the palm strike forces his sight upward, obscuring his view, "collapse" forward into an upward elbow strike.

With his view suddenly forced upward, your foe doesn't see the shadowhand elbow blow that immediately follows your chin strike. (See Figure 32.)

This advantageous position also allows you to perform other follow-up strikes in rapid succession (Figure 33). For example, you can easily augment your chin strike/rising elbow strike with an unseen rising knee strike (targeting groin, lower abdomen).

Likewise, you can follow up your chin-strike/elbow combination with a tiger-claw strike to your foe's face and/or with a hair/head grab that forces his head down into your (unseen) rising knee.

Shadowhand Combinations

Shadowhanders also use combinations of coordinated blocks and strikes to overcome an opponent. Many of these combinations are created by pairing *ukemi* methods of movement with the collapsing principle, which in turn is paired with deceptive oblique shadowhand strikes.

Using the collapsing principle, you can strike a foe with a rapid-fire "four-point set" attack composed of a crescent punch followed by an inward horizontal elbow strike, followed by an outward (reverse) horizontal elbow strike, followed by a horizontal backfist, all targeting your foe's head, all striking within the space of a heartbeat.

When performed correctly, the fourth strike (backfist) of this right-side crescent punch combo hides from sight the left punch that begins your follow-up left-side crescent punch combo.

(NOTE: When done smoothly, this crescent punch combination allows you to strike your foe with a flurry of blows, all in rapid succession (i.e., left punch, left elbow strike, reverse left elbow strike, left backfist strike, right punch, right elbow strike.)

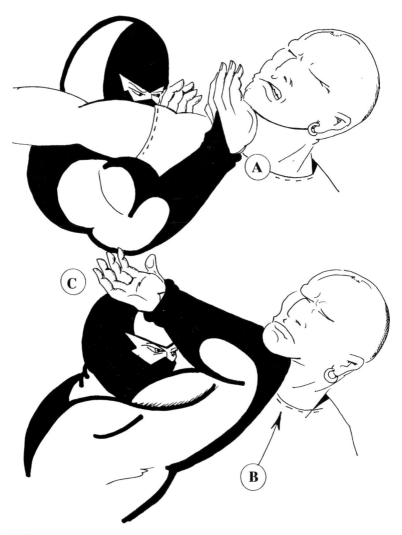

FIGURE 32: RISING SUN COMBINATION

A. *Having slipped to the outside of your foe's attacking lead hand, counter-strike up and inside to his centerline (See Figure 31).*

B. *Having struck with your hand (e.g., rising palm, uppercut), continue your forward attack momentum by "collapsing" forward into a vertical rising elbow strike.*

C. *Your rising elbow strike places your hand in position for follow-up/finishing-off strikes (see Figure 33).*

FIGURE 33: RISING SUN FOLLOW-UP STRIKES

A. *Descending elbow strike (targeting back of head, spine).*

B. *Rising knee strike (targeting groin, abdomen, face).*

C. *Turn (completed) rising knee strike into stomp or thrusting kick (see Figure 39).*

This combination is coordinated with moving forward in the half-moon step. (See Figures 34 and 35.)

Low Blows

Many shadowhand strikes require dropping under a foe's line-of-sight attack, rather than forcing his sight up (as in Figures 32 and 33).

For example, moving forward and down using the Chinese squat" (Figure 26) allows you to strike up into a foe's face or solar plexus, or down into his groin and lower body with various hammer blows and clawing strikes.

One shadowhand technique calls for performing the Chinese squat while striking high to your foe's face in order to draw his attention away from the fact that you have hooked your cross-over foot behind his leading foot, allowing you to sweep him to the ground as you pull back. (See Figures 36 and 37.)

(NOTE: This same type of pull-back sweep can be used anytime you can position your leading foot behind your opponent's leading foot.)

Arch-Escape Striking

Having successfully maneuvered into the arch-escape position (Figure 27), you can then strike back into a foe's centerline (solar plexus, abdomen, groin) and into his lower body (knees, shin, instep) with a variety of techniques, including

- hammerfist to groin
- horizontal elbow strike to solar plexus (moving in with slight squat)
- rear thrust-kick targeting the midsection
- backward sweeping kick-back throw, sweeping out your foe's leading leg

(NOTE: This position can also be used for launching a counterstrike against a knife-wielding attacker—see the kobudo-jutsu section.)

See Figure 38.

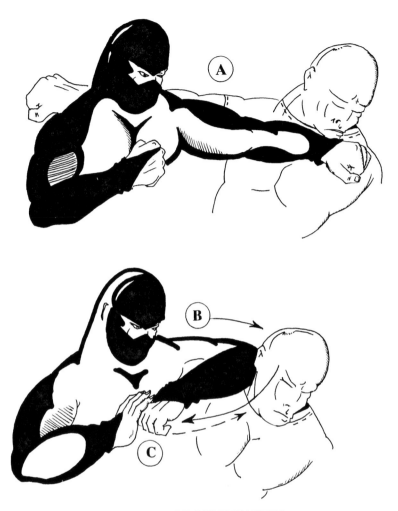

FIGURE 34: CRESCENT PUNCH COMBINATION

A. *Having slipped inside your foe's leading arm attack, counter with a straight punch.*

B. *Continue your attacking momentum by "collapsing" into an inward elbow strike.*

C. *Successful completion of the elbow strike places you in perfect position for continuing your counterattack on the opposite side of your body (see Figure 35).*

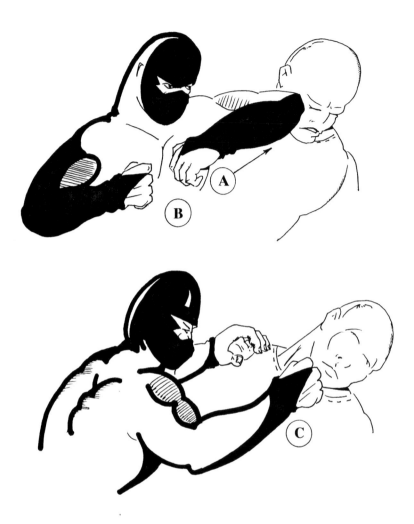

FIGURE 35: CRESCENT PUNCH FOLLOW-UP STRIKING

A. *Having completed the crescent punch (lead-punch/elbow strike) combination, immediately reverse direction and strike back into your foe's face with a rear (outward) elbow strike.*

B. *Immediately upon striking with your elbow, "unfurl" a backfist strike.*

C. *Your elbow strike and accompanying backfist strike hides your right-side "shadowhand," allowing you to begin your striking "set" again from Figure 34.*

FIGURE 36: LOW INSIDE ATTACK

A. *Dropping into the Chinese squat (Figure 26) under your foe's attacking lead hand,*

B. *strike in to your foe's centerline.*

C. *Correctly performing the Chinese squat places your rear foot behind your foe's leading foot.*

FIGURE 37: PULL-BACK SWEEP

A. *Having counterattacked into your foe's centerline by positioning yourself in the Chinese squat, upset his balance by striking into his upper body (face, throat, chest) with a palm strike.*

B. *Simultaneously with your palm strike on his upper body, pull forward with your rear foot, sweeping your foe's leading foot.*

FIGURE 38: ARCH-ESCAPE STRIKING

A. *Having successfully blocked your foe's attacking hand with your leading hand (see Fig. 27), pass his blocked hand off your second hand.*

B. *Having passed under the arch created by having blocked your foe's attacking arm, employ the switch-back pivot (Fig. 22) to move into your foe's centerline.*

C. *Counterattack into your foe's centerline with a variety of hand (hammerfist, tiger's claw) and foot (rear thrust kick) strikes and/or with a kickback sweep.*

Striking with the Feet

The average untrained fighter can kick with more than 165 pounds of force. There is no limit to the amount of force a trained kickfighter can muster. It only takes 40 pounds of force to break a knee. Consequently, leg weapons (hips, knees, shins, feet) have always held a respected place in the shadowhand arsenal.

Shadowhanders apply the same rules to using feet as weapons as they do to using hand weapons. They first use *ukemi* methods of movement to place themselves in position for initiating their counterattack. All shadowhand methods of movement contain hidden techniques (e.g., sweeps, strikes) that automatically work when the method of movement is performed correctly. Thus, proper attention to *ukemi* places the shadowhander in a prime position where oblique and hidden shadowhand finishing-off techniques work by themselves.

Kicks and the Collapsing Principle

Shadowhanders use the collapsing principle to defeat a foe attempting to counter their kicks. Thus, when your close-in rising-knee strike is jammed by your foe, instantly employ the collapsing principle and, rather than withdraw and rechamber your attacking leg, reroute the knee strike by turning it into a side-thrust kick targeting your foe's lower body (Figure 39).

Hidden Kicks

Many shadowhand ukemi contain hidden kicking strikes. For example, the half-moon step, when used correctly and forcefully, automatically transforms into an efficient sweeping technique and/or a devastating hook-kick strike (Figure 40).

A kick also hides within the over-the-fence pivot (Figure 21). Spinning into the over-the-fence, instead of placing your raised leading foot down into a horse stance, you continue with the raised leg's arc outward, which transforms into a forceful outside crescent kick (Figure 41).

Likewise, the horse-stance shift (Figure 24) can be used for spinning into a foe, for example, counterattacking with a thrust kick to a foe's midsection (Figure 42).

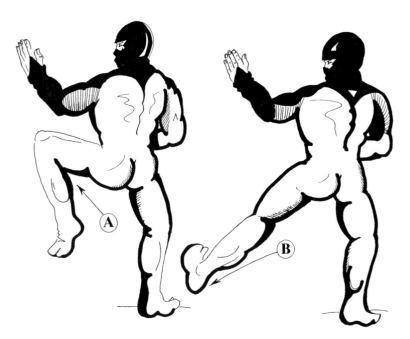

**FIGURE 39: COLLAPSING PRINCIPLE
(KNEE BECOMES THRUST-KICK)**

A. *As your leading knee comes up (either to perform a rising knee strike or in preparation for a front kick), it is jammed by your foe. . . .*

B. *Rather than retracting your rising knee, continue your attack momentum by rotating your hip forward and performing a low-level side-thrust-kick (targeting your foe's knee, shin, or instep).*

Additional Unarmed Strikes

Beyond their hands and feet, shadowhanders have at their disposal a multitude of additional unarmed striking weapons. These additional weapons are easy to find; simply follow the collapsing principle (see Figure 30).

Turtle's Head

The hard bones of the wrist (carpals) make an excellent striking surface, especially for fighters with smaller hands (e.g., women).

Also known as a bent-wrist strike, the turtle's-head blow can

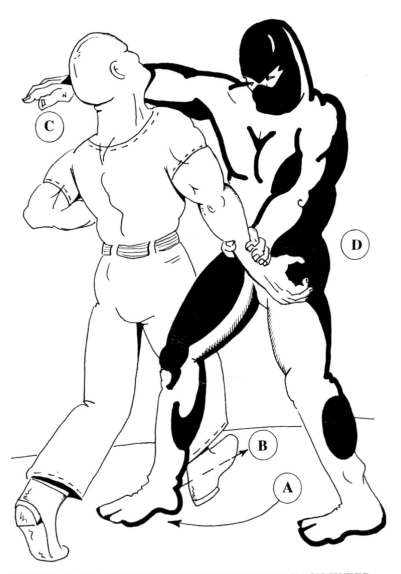

FIGURE 40: HALF-MOON STEP BECOMES KICK-BACK SWEEP

A. *Having slipped your foe's leading hand attack, step forward forcefully with your half-moon step.*

B. *As your half-moon step comes down directly behind your foe's leading leg, kick backward, sweeping his lead leg.*

C. *Augment your takedown by pushing (C) or pulling (D) at your foe's upper body.*

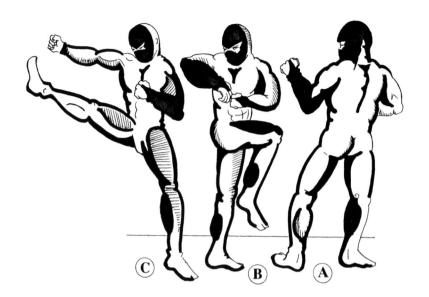

FIGURE 41: OVER-THE-FENCE INTO CRESCENT KICK

A. *Beginning in a left leading horse stance . . .*

B. *perform an over-the-fence pivot (see Figure 21).*

C. *Completing your pivot, rather than lowering your leading leg, whip your leading leg outward in a crescent, targeting your foe with the side of your leading foot.*

be used for striking "hard" targets (temple, chin, base of the skull) as well as for penetrating "soft" targets (solar plexus, groin).

One of the best shadowhand striking techniques employs the turtle's head in a block-strike combination (Figure 43).

This double turtle's-head strike is a perfect shadowhand technique in the way it deliberately distracts the eye with the forward blocking turtle's head. Thus your foe never sees the second turtle's head—coming up simultaneously and obliquely on the outside—that strikes into the back of the head. As a finishing-off move, the first (blocking) turtle's head instantly reverses its path, swinging back into the foe's head after your first blow has stunned and/or forced your foe's head forward (further obscuring his LOS).

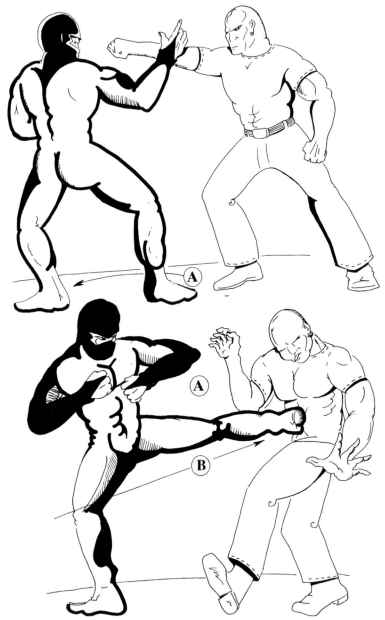

FIGURE 42: HORSE-STANCE SHIFT

A. *Continuing your spinning momentum, spin 180 degrees into your foe's centerline . . .*

B. *Counterattacking with a side-thrust-kick targeting his groin and/or abdomen.*

FIGURE 43: DOUBLE TURTLE'S HEAD

A. *Faced with a right punching attack, step back into a horse stance and block-strike into your foe's leading hand with your right bent wrist (turtle's head).*

B. *Simultaneously with your turning inward to block your foe's lead hand, your left turtle's head comes around to strike your foe's head (temple, back of head). (NOTE: Your foe's eyes will follow your first blocking turtle's head, and he will never see your second shadowhand turtle's-head blow coming.)*

C. *Immediately upon striking your foe with your second (left) turtle's-head blow, reverse the direction of your first (right) blocking-striking turtle's head and strike him with a third turtle's-head blow to the other side of his head.*

Forearm Blows

During close-quarters combat, the radius bone of the forearm can be pressed into a foe's larynx to both pin and/or strangle him.

—Dr. Haha Lung
The Ancient Art of Strangulation, 1995

The forearm can also be used for applying arms locks (i.e., pressing down on the elbow) and for trapping and/or breaking a foe's knee (Figure 44).

The Short Wing

Elbows are very versatile weapons, good for blocking and trapping as well as for devastating strikes from several angles. Short-wing elbow strikes also easily lend themselves to combination striking. (See Figures 45–48.)

Some martial arts, for example, wing chung kung fu and crane-style kung fu, emphasize effective use of the short wing for both blocking and striking.

Anytime a solid punch makes contact, or even when a foe succeeds in deflecting one of your punches, the shadowhand collapsing principle allows you to continue your forward momentum by turning your attacking arm into a short-wing strike.

When used for blocking, the short wing is the second line of defense after an attacker has "slipped" past the shadowhander's initial blocking hand and/or has closed with him. The short wing is used to "tip" an incoming punch, thus creating an opening for your counterattack.

The short wing can also be used as both a simultaneous block-strike, both blocking and damaging a foe's attacking arm (or foot) by striking into a his attacking arm and/or down into his trapped leg (after having trapped his kicking leg).

The short wing can also be used for trapping a foe's extended attacking arm, setting him up for finishing-off strikes.

FIGURE 44: FOREARM BLOWS/FOREARM LEG BAR

A. *Having moved in close with your foe by blocking his attacking arm up and out, strike into his midsection with a horizontal elbow strike.*

B. *Slide down his midsection until your forearm "locks out" his knee. Augment this leg lock ("bar") by pulling his lower leg (calf) toward you while pressing your forearm into his knee.*
(NOTE: Performed forcefully, this technique can break the knee.)

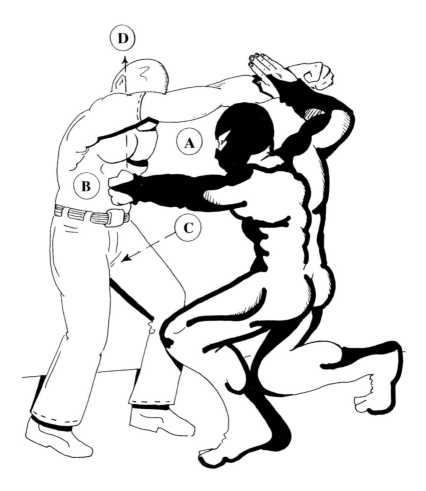

FIGURE 45: SHORT-WING COLLAPSING PRINCIPLE COMBINATION

A. *Having blocked your foe's attacking lead arm,*
B. *strike into his centerline with a straight punch or with a solid palm blow targeting his solar plexus.*
C. *Immediately upon making solid contact with your punch, lower your weight, "collapsing" forward into a descending vertical elbow strike targeting his groin and/or bladder area.*
D. *Follow up your strike to his groin by striking upward with a palm strike (targeting your foe's chin).*

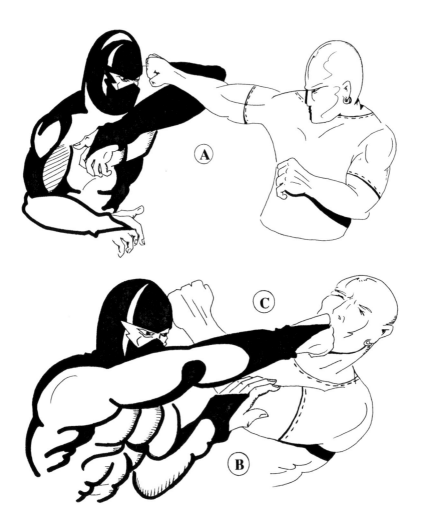

FIGURE 46: SHORT-WING DOUBLE BLOCK COMBINATION

A. *As your foe punches forward with his right hand, "tip" his attacking hand inward with your short wing (elbow).*

B. *As your foe throws his second (left-hand) punch, your short wing reverses its direction, trapping his second punch against his body.*

C. *With his two arms trapped, counterstrike into his face.*

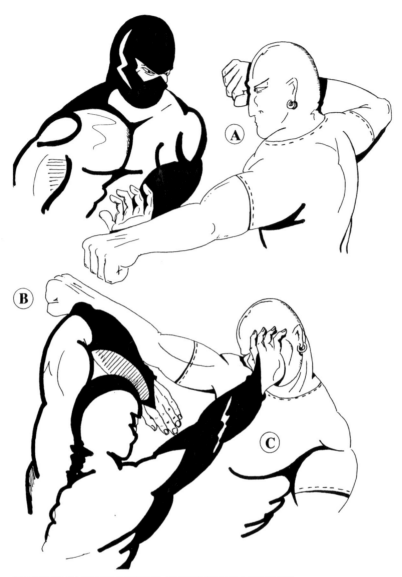

FIGURE 47: SHORT-WING COUNTERSTRIKING I

A. *As your foe strikes forward with a left leading punch, counter with a left cross-body block.*

B. *As your foe throws his second (right) punch, counter with a left reverse elbow strike directly into his attacking arm.*

C. *Having countered your foe's "one-two" punch, you can now counterstrike into his face with your right.*

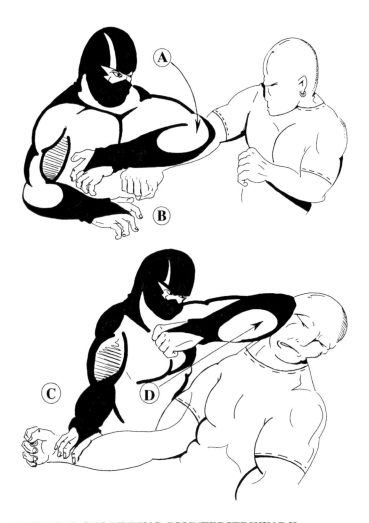

FIGURE 48: SHORT-WING COUNTERSTRIKING II

A. *As your foe attacks with a right leading punch, you step back using the horse-stance shift (Figure 24), while your left short wing comes up and over the punching arm, in effect, "smothering" the punch.*

B. *Your left short wing forces your foe's attacking arm into your waiting right hand.*

C. *Your right hand seizes hold of your foe's deflected punching arm, while*

D. *you simultaneously reverse the direction of your short wing, attacking back into your foe's upper body (face, throat) with a reverse (outward) elbow strike.*

(NOTE: Use your hold on your foe's leading hand to pull him into your reverse elbow, thus doubling the impact of the strike.)

Shoulder

In the water section of his *A Book of Five Rings*, Musashi teaches the use of the "body strike," wherein you "turn your face to the side and strike the foe's chest (centerline) with your thrusting left shoulder."

Samurai used this technique to unbalance and stun their foes in preparation for cutting them down with a weapon.

Musashi assures the reader that the body strike, done properly, can knock a foe 10 to 20 feet, and that it is even possible to kill a foe by continuously striking him with this technique.

Head Butt

If you've ever seen a *tameshiwara* breaking demonstration, one where a karateka uses his head to crush a stack of bricks or a ton of ice, you will no longer have any doubts as to the effectiveness of striking with the head. (See Figure 49.)

In both defensive and offensive situations—e.g., striking forward as part of an offensive-attack "set" or snapping your head backward (to escape a grab from behind)—the head is an effective weapon.

Head butts can also be used in combination striking.

Hips

See the section on jutaijutsu below.

Shin

Professional kick-boxers deaden the nerves in their shins in order to better withstand an opponent's kicks. While necessary

---

FIGURE 49: HEAD-BUTTING

A. *Having successfully closed with your foe, pin his arms at his sides to prevent his punching.*

B. *Using the forward momentum of closing with your foe, drive your head forcefully into his solar plexus.*

C. *Immediately upon head-butting into your foe's solar plexus, drive your head up into his chin and/or downward-turned face. (NOTE: Your foe's face will be turned downward as a result of your having struck him in the solar plexus.)*

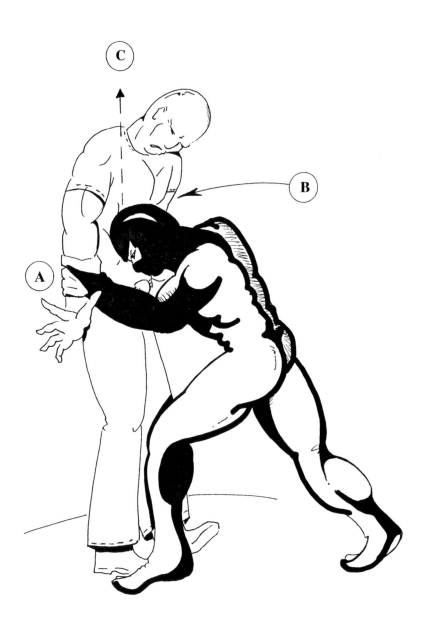

for professional fighters, spending hours beating your shins against a tree is not required of most people. Even without such conditioning, shins can be used for both blocking and striking. For example, a shin kick into a foe's thigh can cripple his attack. A rising shin can be used to deflect a low-level kick, rather than intercepting its full force with a solid block.

Jutaijutsu (Grappling)

When near, make it appear you are far away. When far away, make it appear you are near.

—Sun Tzu

Danger increases with proximity. Simply put, the farther away from a foe you can remain while still effectively striking him, the safer you generally are.

In realistic, combat-oriented martial arts, for example in American zendokan-ryu taijutsu, pioneered by Shihan Peter Gilbert in the 1970s, students train to respond instantly to a "dire threat situation" with the "three parameters."

Faced with an attacking foe, their first line of defense and offense is kobudo-jutsu, the use of weapons. These weapons can be traditional weapons (e.g., gun, knife, Mace) they've brought to the fray or "environmental weapons," everyday objects gleaned from their surroundings (Omar 1993).

When unable to secure a weapon (which is seldom the case!), shadowhanders unleash a flurry of daikentaijutsu hand strikes, kicks, and other damaging blocks and blows.

Last, when forced into closing with a foe, shadowhanders employ jutaijutsu grappling techniques to unbalance a foe and then take him down and keep him there.

Like most "rules of thumb," the three parameters do not apply in 100 percent of situations.

There are, in fact, times when being in close to an enemy is advantageous. For example, a long-armed opponent has trouble punching a smaller, close-in fighter.

Likewise, a small guerrilla force, bold enough to operate right under the bigger army's figurative LOS, is often at an advantage.

The proof is in the pudding.

In both their overall field strategy and their close-quarter combat, the Vietnamese followed the adage of "grasping tight the belt," that is, staying close to their foes. In field operations, this made it more difficult for the French, and later the Americans, to call in pinpoint air strikes, since at close quarters friend and foe were indistinguishable.

Likewise, when forced into hand-to-hand combat, Vietcong sappers literally "gripped tight the belt," closing with a foe. This often put larger Westerners at a disadvantage, allowing the smaller Vietcong fighters to employ "shadowhand" grappling techniques with devastating effectiveness.

Some martial arts specialize in closing with, unbalancing, and then finishing a foe using combat grappling. Excellent examples of these are Japanese jujutsu and aikido and the Russian sambo.

For shadowhanders as well, being close to a foe helps disguise their deceptive movements and further masks already oblique follow-up strikes. As already mentioned, shadowhanders nurture their proximity body sense as a vital skill, both for fighting in pitch darkness or for fighting when temporarily blinded (e.g., by dirt, Mace, tobacco juice, beer).

This sort of bodily awareness is vital, especially when you find yourself locked in a hand-to-hand struggle, when you need to be able to "feel" your opponent shifting his weight (in preparation for a throw). You also have to be able to "sense" when your opponent is maneuvering his arm into position to apply a lock or a choke hold.

Likewise, when a fight goes to the ground, you need to have a body awareness of your foe jockeying for position.

Hidden within each shadowhand ukemi foot movement are inherent sweeps and strikes.

Hidden Sweeps

Any time you perform the half-moon step (Figure 20) correctly, it places your leading foot behind your foe's leading foot, allowing you to sweep him to the ground—where you then have the option of escaping or finishing him off with stomps (see Figure 40)—in the same way the "over-the-fence" pivot (Figure 21) can be turned into a fight-ending sweep. (NOTE: Thrusting your hips and/or buttocks into an opponent is an excellent way to unbalance him. Jamming your hips into and under the level of an opponent's hips is the basis of many jujutsu throws.) (See Figure 50.)

The horse-stance shift (Figure 24) can also be transformed into a takedown sweep. Having pivoted away from a foe's punching attack, continue your circular movement and momentum by dropping low into an "iron broom sweep." (See Figure 51.)

Moving into a foe with a Chinese squat, you execute a hand strike to his upper body, which masks your lead foot placing itself behind his lead-foot ankle. This position allows you to topple him as you pull back (see Figure 37).

When grappling with a foe, create an "arch escape" (Figure 52) by raising your "short wing."

As soon as this "arch" appears, you can "escape" through it before pivoting into a "Kick-back" sweep (see Figure 38).

Hidden Throws

A front "thrust kick" to the midsection can easily be turned into a "wheel throw" (aka "circle throw").

Shadowhanders then add an additional roll-over move to this takedown—an unexpected move that places them on top the thrown foe, an advantageous position from which to finish off a foe already disoriented from the takedown. (See Figure 53.)

(NOTE: Never let go of a foe you have successfully thrown, since this will allow him to break his fall and escape by rolling out and away from you, as shadowhanders train to do! Instead, always follow a thrown foe to the ground, finishing him with a coup-de-grace hand blow or with stomps.)

The Chinese squat can easily be used to set up a pivoting "pull-down throw."

Other jutaijutsu throws can be built on—and found hidden in—the switchback pivot described earlier in Figure 22.) (See Figure 54, p. 122).

FIGURE 50: "OVER THE FENCE" BECOMES SWEEP

A. *Successfully completing the over-the-fence movement (Figure 21) close to a foe automatically places your lead foot down behind your foe's, allowing you to easily employ a hip throw and/or sweep him to the ground.*

B. *Augment unbalancing your foe by grabbing/striking into his upper body. (NOTE: Thrusting your hips (and/or buttocks) into an opponent is an excellent way to unbalance him. Jamming your hips into and under the level of an opponent's hips is the basis of many jujutsu throws.)*

FIGURE 51: HORSE STANCE BECOMES "IRON BROOM" SWEEP

A. *Having successfully avoided your foe's punching attack by stepping back into a horse-stance shift (Figure 24), continue your turn 180 degrees, dropping your hands to the ground as you extend your leading leg into the "iron broom" position, sweeping your foe's leg(s) out from under him.*

B. *Shadowhand rule: Anytime you place your hands on the ground, fill your hands with dirt, stones, etc. that can be thrown into your foe's eyes as you rise.*

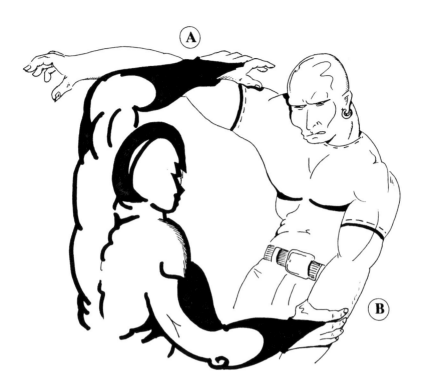

FIGURE 52: CREATING THE ARCH DURING GRAPPLING

A. *Having closed with a foe, create "the arch" (see Figure 27) by positioning your "short wing" under your foe's grasping arm and lifting.*

B. *Creating the arch during grappling is made easier when you use jutaijutsu "push-pull" to distract your foe by aiming knee strikes at his groin and/or targeting his legs and feet with short kicks and stomps.*

FIGURE 53: "WHEEL THROW" ROLL-OVER

A. *Closing with your foe, strike into his midsection with a front thrusting kick.*

B. *Retaining your grip on your foe, your foot firmly planted in his midsection, "collapse" backward, carrying your foe down and over your prone body.*

C. *Rather than releasing your falling foe, follow him over, rolling on top of him as he lands and pinning his arms with your legs as you straddle his midsection.*

D. *Finish your already disoriented foe with hand blows.*

Kobudo-Jutsu (Weapons Use)

It is dangerous for warriors to have likes and dislikes. . . . Do not move one foot preferentially.

—Miyamoto Musashi

Miyamoto Musashi warns that you should never have a favorite weapon. Primarily, this is because favoring one weapon over another limits you to predictable ways of moving. For example, you move differently when stabbing forward with a knife than you do when swinging a heavy bludgeon such as a baseball bat. Over time, repeated movements become habit. Unexamined habit can get you killed.

Second, your being known to favor one style of fighting over another alerts an enemy beforehand, giving him advance warning for developing effective countermeasures against you. This is why professional fighters (e.g., boxers) study past fight tapes of their opponents before ever stepping in the ring with them.

It is mandatory that shadowhanders learn weapons.

The more familiar you are with the various types of weapons, the more conversant you are with their use, the more options you will have when it comes to (1) surviving an attack from such weapons and (2) being able to call upon such weapons in your own defense, without telegraphing your intention and arsenal to your enemy.

FIGURE 54: SWITCH-BACK THROW

A. *As your foe lunges forward with an overhead attack, your hands come up to block.*

B. *You simultaneously step forward with your right leading foot.*

C. *Having successfully blocked the overhead attack, seize your foe's arm and suddenly pivot using a switch-back (see Figure 22).*

D. *As you do the switch-back pivot, kneel on your leading leg, flipping your already unbalanced foe down and over.*

Most important, the more you know about conventional and traditional weapons, the easier it will be—in an emergency—for you to find, or quickly manufacture, similar "environmental weapon" substitutes.

The shadowhand kobudo-jutsu techniques that follow are built on the previous taijutsu skills you've acquired (e.g., ukemi, the collapsing principle). To this, you add an unhealthy dose (unhealthy for your foes, that is!) of shadowhand subtlety and subterfuge, all designed to further help you unnerve, unbalance, and then take out a foe.

Hiding Your Hand

Forewarned is forearmed.

Mastery of shadowhand kobudo-jutsu begins with learning how to carry your weapons undetected. (Review Disguising Your Intention, Chapter 6.)

If an enemy sees you openly brandishing a weapon he will, of course, become alarmed and be forewarned of your "evil" intent.

Even modern street punks know how to hide their weapons in order to approach their mugging victims without alarming them.

In a battlefield situation, the weapons a commander brings to the battlefield can alert rival commanders to the type of strategy he can be expected to deploy.

Musashi followed his own advice about not tipping your tactical hand by having a favorite weapon. Still considered the greatest Japanese swordsman ever, it is ironic that Musashi won his greatest battles without swords. At age 13, Musashi beat an adult samurai to death with a bludgeon. Many times over the years, Musashi defeated armed foes by using only wooden swords, once using a stick he was cutting to make a bow. Musashi is also credited with defeating foes by using a tree limb, a tanto knife, or a fan. In his most celebrated victory, Musashi killed Japan's "second greatest" swordsman in 1612 by crushing his skull with a rowboat oar!

Shadow Weapons

Miyamoto Musashi was an expert at "hiding his hand." At one point, he reportedly mastered the art of kakashi-jutsu, as taught by the emmei-ryu school of martial arts. Kakashi-jutsu is a ninja art specializing in the use of small lethal weapons. These weapons—easily concealed, often in the palm of the hand—include such things as small knives, poisoned dirks, and throwing stars, as well as a host of "environmental weapons." (See Figure 55.)

Kakashi-jutsu includes training in use of the *jo* and *yawara* (short sticks), as well as mastery of the iron fan and the easily concealed *manriki* ("10,000 strength chain"). (See Figure 56.)

"Hiding your hand" thus refers to either (1) convincing an enemy that you have a weapon when you don't or (2) not letting an enemy know you are carrying a weapon when you are.

The first goal can be accomplished through clever use of silhouette and sleight of hand designed to trick a foe's eye and keep him guessing.

FIGURE 55: SHADOW WEAPONS
TONKI **(EASILY CONCEALED)**

FIGURE 56: SHADOW WEAPONS, *MANRIKI*

In March 1934, outlaw John Dillinger escaped from the Crown Point, Indiana, jail by quickly flashing a piece of soap (some say a piece of wood) that he'd carved into the crude shape of a pistol.

Times have changed, but our eyes and the way our brains process information hasn't. Fast forward 63 years to the Kansas State Prison, where in January 1997 another outlaw used the exact same ploy to escape.

We often hear stories of innocent people shot dead by police who—seeing the "suspect" in silhouette or heavy shadow—mistakenly believe the suspect is holding a pistol or a rifle, only to discover later that their victim was holding a drill or a broom.

Shadowhanders know this failing of the human eye and brain and use it to their advantage, often convincing a foe that they have a weapon when in fact they are unarmed.

The second goal of "hiding your hand," keeping a foe from realizing you're carrying a weapon, is accomplished by either (1) disguising your weapon and/or (2) disguising the fact that you are carrying and/or reaching for that weapon.

No one was better at hiding the fact that they were carrying weapons than medieval ninja.

All too often samurai of that era learned a fatal lesson about a harmless-looking, apparently unarmed monk's being anything but a monk, everything but unarmed and harmless! (See Figure 57.)

Today, shadowhanders can apply the same principles as those medieval ninja by choosing their wardrobe to ensure that while appearing unarmed, they are actually "packing" a multitude of "environmental weapons."

More important, even if you do not choose to deliberately "arm" yourself with such weapons, nor to embrace such ploys, still—for safety's sake—you must make yourself more aware of those around you who might choose to study and so arm themselves. Take, for example, that staggering drunk approaching you—the one busy gulping down his last swallow of cheap wine, his other hand dangling lax at his side. Like the medieval monk, surely he is no threat? (See Figures 58 and 59.)

Another way to disguise the fact that you are carrying "shadow weapons" is by using your body to block your foe's view. Whether you are wielding traditional weapons or makeshift environmental weapons, the shadowhand principles of concealment and use remain the same. For example, the "inside grip" favored by knife fighters because it hides the blade from a foe's sight can just as easily be used to hide the fact that you are holding a pair of nunchaku or a screwdriver at the ready (Figures 60 and 61).

Knife fighters often keep their forward (blocking) hand moving in front of their rear knife hand in a position known to shadowhanders as the "dancing hand blind." Each time the knife "disappears" behind the forward hand and then "reappears," your foe's mind is forced to refocus, further unnerving a foe trying to keep track of your blade (Figure 62).

FIGURE 57: "SHADOW WEAPONS" (MEDIEVAL)

A . *Fan weapon, used for distracting (see Figure 13). Some ninja fans are made of metal and/or lined with razor-sharp edges.*

B. *Hat, used for distraction. Often reinforced with metal weaving for use as shield. Often equipped with razor-sharp edges.*

C. *Prayer beads, made of metal. Used for fighting, strangling, climbing, etc.*

D. *Bo-staff could be used for fighting. Metal point could quickly be affixed to end to make deadly spear.*

E. *Hidden scoop at end of staff used for flinging sand and small stones into a foe's eyes.*

F. *Hollow staff could easily hide myriad weapons: blades, nunchaku, chained weapons. Hollowed-out staff could also be used as a blow gun or under-water breathing tube. Reinforced staffs could be used as climbing aids.*

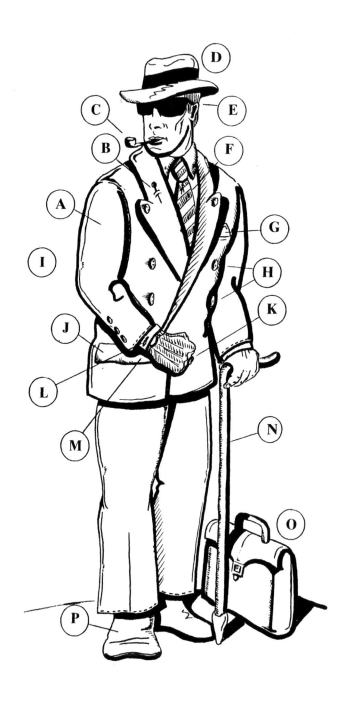

FIGURE 58: SHADOW WEAPONS—MODERN MAN

A. Jackets and coats can be wrapped around the arm as protection against knife/bludgeon attacks. Reversible jackets can help you elude pursuit. A jacket, strategically placed, can make a foe unsure of your position or direction of movement (see Figures 28 and 29).

B. Stick-pins and small lapel pins can be used to stab an attacker. Such pins can be augmented with poisons. Increasingly, such small objects can carry cameras and listening devices.

C. Pipes can be used to stab into a foe's eyes. A burning cigarette can be flicked at a foe to startle. Smoke can be blown into a foe's eyes, or ashes thrown into his eyes.

D. Hats can be used to blind a foe's line of sight (see Figure 13). Hats can also be used to cover the hand when fighting off a knife-wielding attacker. Gang-bangers often augment their caps by sewing razor blades into the brims.

E. Glasses can be used for stabbing into a foe's throat, etc. In a survival situation, glass lenses are used for signaling and for starting emergency fires.

F. Ties can be used to strangle. Heavier objects can be tied to the ends of such "flex-ible weapons" to create nunchaku and bludgeons. Ties can also be used as aids to climbing and for tying up a defeated foe.

G. Handkerchiefs can be used in the same way as ties and belts. Heavy objects (e.g., pool ball, stone) can be tied into a handkerchief for use as a spinning bludgeon. A small screw, tied into the end of a handkerchief, becomes a "snapping" weapon.

H. Buttons can be thrown at a foe to startle. Such small objects can also be thrown to distract a sentry's attention.

I. Belts can be used in the same ways as ties and handkerchiefs. In addition, belts with heavy buckles (e.g., "biker chain belts") can be used as bludgeons and/or wrapped around the hand to augment punching. There are specialized belts available that contain myriad weapons, from knives to derringers.

J. Pockets can be filled with tonki, easily concealed small objects used as weapons (see Figure 55).

K. Rings of various sorts can augment punching. Rings with large faces can also be turned around to augment palm strikes.

L. Cufflinks (see stick-pins above).

M. Wristwatches can be slipped over the hand (like brass knuckles) to augment punching. The shiny surfaces of watches can be used for signaling in a survival situation. The glass in a watch can be used to start fires.

N. Canes can be used for a variety of defensive and offensive actions (see Figure 68). Specialized canes are available containing swords, firearms, tear gas, stun guns, etc.

O. Briefcases, suitcases, and purses can all be used as defensive shields when fight-ing off an attacker. These cases can also hide myriad useful tools and weapons. Specialized cases and purses are available that, with the press of a button, con-vert into firearms. Other cases contain stun guns in easily detachable handles.

P. Shoes can be slipped over the hand for use in defensive situations. Heavy shoes can be used as bludgeons, either held in the hand or swung by the strings. The laces in shoes can be used in the same way as ties, handkerchiefs, and belts. Street-gang members often augment their shoes with protruding spikes and con-cealed razors.

FIGURE 59: SHADOW WEAPONS—MODERN WOMAN

A. *Wigs can be used in much the same way as hats. Switching wigs can help you elude pursuers. Wigs can be set afire and thrown into the face of an attacker. Wigs can be placed over the hand to guard against a knife attack. A wig can be placed in a strategic spot to make a pursuer believe you are someplace you are not.*

B. *Hats (see Figure 58).*

C. *Earrings and other small objects can be used as* tonki.

D. *Necklaces, brooches, and other adornments can also be used as* tonki. *Increasingly, such small objects are being used to conceal small cameras and/or listening devices.*

E. *Rings (see Figure 58).*

F. *Purses can hide myriad weapons (e.g., aerosols, spike-handled combs). The purses themselves can be used as shields. Heavy purses can be swung bludgeon-like on their straps.*

G. *Slacks are always more "fighter-friendly" than skirts.*

H. *Shoes (see Figure 58).*

I. *Pantyhose can be used in much the same way as ties, belts, handkerchiefs, etc. (see Figure 58).*

J. *Belts (see Figure 58).*

K. *Umbrellas can be used in the same way as canes. Like canes, specialized umbrellas come equipped with stun guns, swords, or even firearms.*

L. *Watches (see Figure 58).*

M. *Jackets (see Figure 58).*

FIGURE 60: DISGUISING WEAPONS

    *A. Your foe hides a knife at the ready inside a paper
bag shaped to look like it contains a bottle.*

    *B. Pulling his hand farther up his sleeve, your foe carries
his blade at the ready by hiding it in his extended glove.*

FIGURE 61: INSIDE GRIP HIDES WEAPONS

FIGURE 62: DANCING HAND BLIND

When it comes to drawing your blade (or substitute environmental weapon), your foe will expect you to pull it from your belt or back pocket. Hiding it, for instance, in your boot or strapped to your calf can allow you to pull your blade while your movement is shielded by your leg (Figure 63).

Likewise, the follow-through movements of the "crescent punch" combination (see Figure 34) can allow you to draw your knife (or other weapon) without your foe realizing you have filled your fist (Figure 64).

Of course, an alternative to bringing your own weapon to the party is to use the weapons your foe generously lets you "borrow" from him. For example, not only can the ukemi arch escape be used to strike your own weapon back into a foe (see Figure 38), but the arch escape can also be used to reroute an attacker's own weapons against him (Figure 65).

Using your body to shield your weapons from your foe's prying eyes works just as well with larger weapons as with smaller weapons such as knives. Ninja (as well as other killer cadres who used swords) became adept at hiding their swords until the last moment, often deliberately baiting a samurai to attack, while never revealing the fact that they were hiding a sword or even a full-length *bo*-staff. For example, a sword can be hidden behind the body by using the same "inside grip" as with a shorter blade.

A full-length sword can also be hidden behind the back, behind the leg, or situated along the spine (Figure 67).

Can't see yourself carrying a sword? What about a cane? The same principle applies for modern shadowhanders disguising the fact that they are hiding a cane, a golf club, or a baseball bat, as for a medieval ninja hiding a sword.

Once you internalize the concept of "shadow weapons," you will be able to "hide" even a full-length *bo*-staff from your foe, striking him before he even suspects you are harboring such a weapon, striking with your shadowhand from angles he never suspected possible. (See Figures 69 and 70.)

Never threaten a foe by brandishing your weapon. When facing an attacker, keep secret the fact that you are holding a weapon to the last possible moment. Fill your fist with the element of surprise. In a kill-or-be-killed situation, your foe should never see the weapon that sends him tumbling into the void!

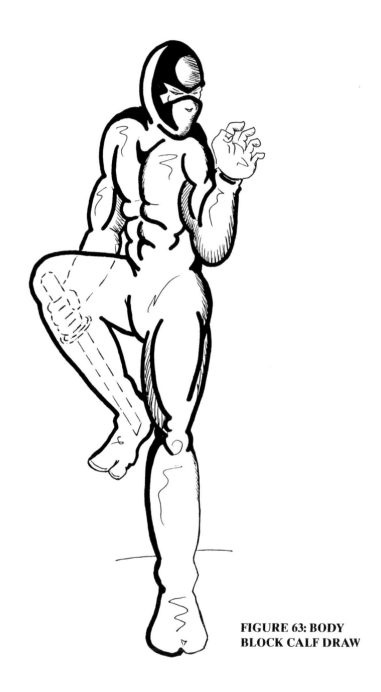

**FIGURE 63: BODY
BLOCK CALF DRAW**

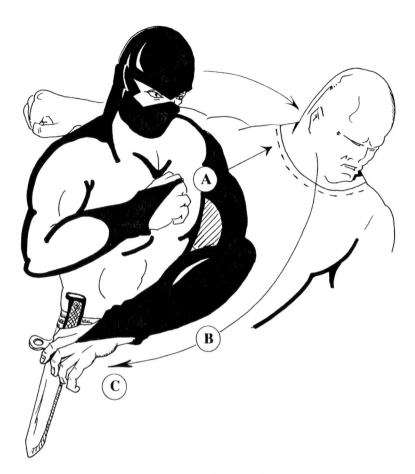

FIGURE 64: FOLLOW-THROUGH KNIFE DRAW

A. Having counterattacked into your foe using the crescent-punch combination (see Figure 34),

B. your hand strikes "through" your foe and continues to the weapon (hidden) at your hip.

C. Following the path of the crescent-punch reverse line of attack, strike back into your foe with your weapon.

FIGURE 65: KNIFE ATTACK REROUTE

A. *Check your foe's overhead knife attack by using the arch-escape blocking position.*

B. *Complete the arch-escape pivot while driving your foe's attacking hand back into his own midsection.*

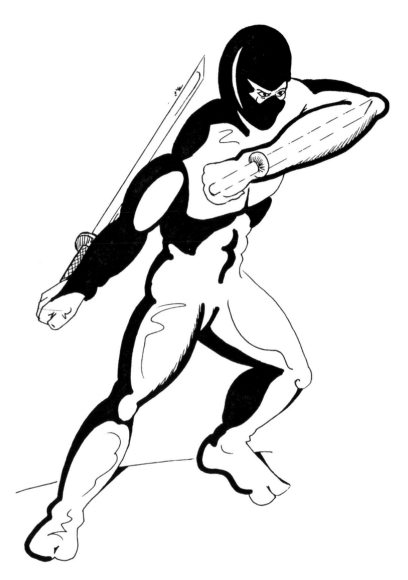

FIGURE 66: BODY SHIELD/SWORD

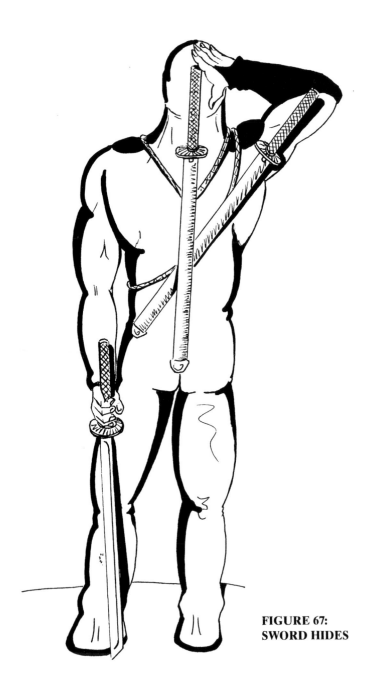

FIGURE 67:
SWORD HIDES

SHADOWHAND

FIGURE 68: BODY SHIELD/MODERN CANE ADAPTATION

A. Your cane remains hidden behind your leg.

B. This allows you to unexpectedly strike up into a foe's groin as he approaches.

FIGURE 69: BODY SHIELD (*BO*-STAFF)

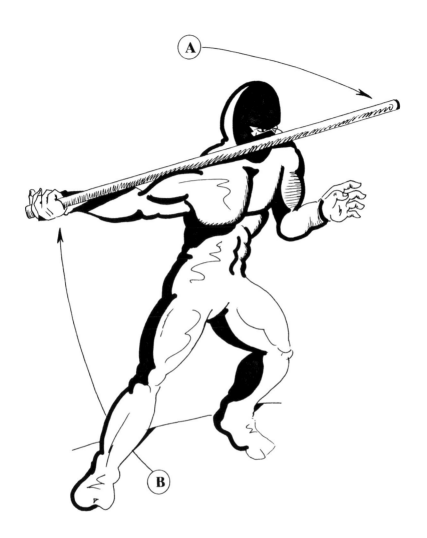

FIGURE 70: EYE-POPPER SHADOWHAND *BO*-STAFF ATTACK

A. Having hidden your bo-staff behind your back,
B. tip it up and forward, over your shoulder, targeting your foe's face and eyes.

Conclusion:
The "Perfect" Weapon

Seek passage without traces.

—Zen adage

Shadowhanders have a saying: *Ki kara saru mo ochiru,* "Even monkeys fall out of trees." In other words, even the best of us stumble, and sometimes bad things happen to good people.

But life is only 10 percent what happens to us. The other 90 percent is how we respond to what happens to us.

How we respond to the curve balls life hurls at us depends in great part on how much "sweat equity" we've invested into prior study—into acquiring those skills and mastering those arts necessary for turning stumbling blocks into stepping stones and, when necessary, sticks into swords.

Any shopping list of such skills must include a diligent study of the martial arts.

Yet, like the all-too-imperfect human beings who developed

the martial arts, no martial art system can lay claim to perfection. Forced to point out perfection on a map, we'd find it situated somewhere the far side of perspiration, just this side of desperation.

Thus shadowhanders have another saying: "The art doesn't make the man; the man makes the art." What this means is that embracing the attitude and application of the shadowhand will not guarantee us 100-percent safety. No martial art can—or should—promise you that.

What giving full attention to the necessity and nuance of the shadowhand will do for you is sharpen your character and hone your will and wits, providing you with an edge your indolent foes lack. This most lethal of edges will allow you to slide past your foe's most guarded of gates like the keenest of dirks slipping between two ribs to touch a fearful heart.

Having successfully penetrated to the heart of your foe's world, you can then choose to leave him broken or—perhaps more mercifully—close your shadowhand tightly around his cowering heart before just as quickly vanishing, taking with you your foe's confidence, his sense of ever feeling safe again, and perhaps his final breath as well!

Ethereal, a master leaves no trace to be seen, mysterious under Heaven, he leaves no sound to be heard. By these two, a master seals his foe's fate.

—Sun Tzu

Bibliography

Higbee, Donna. "Human Invisibility," *Alternate Perceptions* 47 (Winter 1997): 34–36.

Lung, Dr. Haha. *The Ancient Art of Strangulation.* Boulder, Colo.: Paladin Press, 1995.

_____. *Assassin!* Boulder, Colo.: Paladin Press, 1997.

_____. *The Ninja Craft.* Ohio: Alpha Publications, 1997.

_____. *Knights of Darkness.* Boulder, Colo.: Paladin Press, 1998.

Musashi, Miyamoto. *A Book of Five Rings,* misc. translation.

Omar, Ralf Dean. "Ninja Death Touch: The Fact & the Fiction," *Blackbelt* (September 1989).

Omar, Ralf Dean. *Death on Your Doorstep: 101 Weapons in the Home.* Ohio: Alpha Publications, 1993.

Pantanjali. *The Yoga Sutra of Pantanjali*, misc. translation.

Poundstone, William. *Biggest Secrets:* New York: Morrow and Company, 1993

Regardie, Israel. *The Tree of Life.* York Beach, Maine: Samuel Weiser Inc., 1994.

Skinner, Dirk. *Street Ninja.* New York: Barricade Books, 1995.

Sun Tzu. *The Art of War*, misc. translation.

Vankin, Jonathan. *Conspiracies, Cover-ups and Crimes.* Bournemouth, U.K.: Paragon House, 1992.

Vatsyayana. *The Kama Sutra of Vatsyayana.* Translation by Sir Richard Francis Burton, 1995.

Wilson, Colin. *The Supernatural: Mysterious Powers.* London: Aldous Books Ltd., 1975.

About the Authors

Dr. Haha Lung is the author of more than a dozen books on the martial arts and the mysterious cults and killer cadres of the East, including *The Ancient Art of Strangulation* (1995), *Assassin!* (1997), and *Knights of Darkness* (1998), all published by Paladin Press.

Christopher B. Prowant is a noted researcher, author, and martial artist. He currently holds a shodan (black belt) ranking in zendokan-ryu taijutsu and a teaching degree in wan tzu hu chuan (tiger-style kung fu). This is his third book published in collaboration with Dr. Lung.